The Theatre and Its Double

Antonin Artaud

Translated by Victor Corti

ALMA CLASSICS

ALMA CLASSICS LTD
London House
243-253 Lower Mortlake Road
Richmond
Surrey TW9 2LL
United Kingdom
www.almaclassics.com

The Theatre and Its Double first published in French in 1964
First published in Great Britain by Calder & Boyars Ltd in 1970
This revised translation first published by Alma Classics Limited (previously
Oneworld Classics Limited) in 2010. Reprinted August 2011
This new edition first published by Alma Classics Ltd in January 2013

ISBN: 978-1-84749-332-3

Contents

The Theatre and Its Double   1
  Preface: Theatre and Culture   3
  Theatre and the Plague   9
  Production and Metaphysics   23
  Alchemist Theatre   34
  On the Balinese Theatre   38
  Oriental and Western Theatre   49
  No More Masterpieces   53
  Theatre and Cruelty   60
  The Theatre of Cruelty (First Manifesto)   63
  Letters on Cruelty   72
  Letters on Language   75
  The Theatre of Cruelty (Second Manifesto)   88
  An Affective Athleticism   93
  Two Notes   100
  Notes   104

Appendix   115
  Documents Relating to The Theatre and   117
  Its Double
  Notes to the Appendix   149

The Theatre and
Its Double*

Preface: Theatre and Culture*

A T A TIME WHEN LIFE ITSELF is in decline, there has never been so much talk about civilization and culture. And there is a strange correlation between this universal collapse of life at the root of our present-day demoralization and our concern for a culture that has never tallied with life but is made to tyrannize life.

Before saying anything further about culture, I consider the world is hungry and does not care about culture, and people artificially want to turn these thoughts away from hunger and direct them towards culture.

The most pressing thing seems to me not so much to defend a culture whose existence never stopped a man worrying about going hungry or about a better life, but to derive from what we term culture ideas, whose living power is the same as hunger.

Above all, we need to live and believe in what keeps us alive, to believe something keeps us alive, nor should every product of the mysterious recesses of the self be referred back to our grossly creature concerns.

What I mean is this: our immediate need is to eat, but it is even more important not to waste the pure energy of being hungry simply on satisfying that immediate need.

If confusion is a sign of the times, I see a schism between things and words underlying this confusion, between ideas and the signs that represent them.

We are not short of philosophical systems; their number and contradictions are a characteristic of our ancient French and European culture. But where do we see that life, our lives, have been affected by these systems?

I would not go so far as to say philosophical systems ought to be directly or immediately applied, but we ought to choose between the following:

Either these systems are a part of us and we are so steeped in them we live them; therefore, what use are books? Or we are not steeped in

3

them and they are not worth living. In that case what difference would their disappearance make?

I must insist on this idea of an active culture, a kind of second wind growing within us like a new organ, civilization as applied culture, governing even our subtlest acts, the spirit alive in things. The distinction between civilization and culture is artificial, for these two words apply to one and the same act.

We judge a civilized man by the way he behaves – he thinks as he behaves. But we are already confused about the words "civilized man". Everyone regards a cultured, civilized man as someone informed about systems, who thinks in systems, forms, signs and representations.

In other words, a monster who has developed to an absurd degree that faculty of ours for deriving thoughts from actions instead of making actions coincide with thoughts.

If our lives lack fire and fervour, that is to say continual magic, this is because we choose to observe our actions, losing ourselves in meditation on their imagined form, instead of being motivated by them.

This faculty is exclusively human. I would even venture to say it was the infection of humanity which marred ideas that ought to have remained sacred. Far from believing man invented the supernatural and the divine, I think it was man's eternal meddling that ended up in corrupting the divine.

At a time when nothing holds together in life any longer, when we must revise all our ideas about life, this painful separation is the reason why things take revenge on us, and the poetry we no longer have within us and are no longer able to rediscover in things suddenly emerges on the adverse side. Hence the unprecedented number of crimes whose pointless perversity can only be explained by our inability to master life.

Although theatre is made as an outlet for our repressions, a kind of horrible poetry is also expressed in bizarre acts, where changes in the facts of life show its intensity undiminished, needing only to be better directed.

But however we may cry out for magic, at heart we are afraid of pursuing life wholly under the sign of real magic.

Thus our deep-rooted lack of culture is surprised at certain awe-inspiring anomalies; for example, on an island out of contact with present-day civilization, the mere passage of a ship carrying only

4

healthy passengers can induce the outbreak of diseases unknown on that island but peculiar to our countries: shingles, influenza, grippe, rheumatism, sinusitis and polyneuritis.

Similarly, if we think Negroes smell, we are unaware that everywhere except in Europe, we, the whites, smell. I might even say we smell a white smell, white in the same way as we speak of "the whites".

Just as iron turns white-hot, so we could say everything extreme is white. For Asians, white has become a mark of final decomposition.

Having said this, we can begin to form an idea of culture, above all a protest.

A protest against the insane constriction imposed on the idea of culture by reducing it to a kind of incredible Pantheon, producing an idolatry of culture and acting in the same way as idolatrous religions, which put their gods in Pantheons.

A protest against our idea of a separate culture, as if there were culture on the one hand and life on the other, as if true culture were not a rarefied way of understanding and exercising life.

Let them burn down the library at Alexandria. There are powers above and beyond papyri. We may be temporarily deprived of the ability to rediscover these powers, but we will never eliminate their energy. It is also a good thing too many facilities should disappear, and forms ought to be forgotten, then timeless, spaceless culture constrained by our nervous capacities will reappear with renewed energy. And it is only right that cataclysms should occur from time to time, prompting us to return to nature, that is to say, to rediscover life. The old totems – animals, rocks, objects charged with lightning, costumes impregnated with bestiality and everything that serves to catch, tap and direct forces – are dead to us, since we only know how to derive artistic or static profit from them, seeking gratification, not action.

Now totemism acts because it moves, it is made to be enacted. All true culture rests on totemism's primitive, barbarous means, whose wild, that is to say, completely spontaneous life is what I mean to worship.

It was our Western idea of art and the profits we sought to derive from it that made us lose true culture. Art and culture cannot agree, contrary to worldwide usage!

True culture acts through power and exaltation, while the European ideal of art aims to cast us into a frame of mind distinct from the power present in its exaltation. It is a useless, lazy idea and soon leads to death. The Serpent Quetzalcoatl's multiple coils give us a sense of harmony because they express balance, the twists and turns of sleeping power. The intensity of the form is only there to attract and captivate a power which, in music, produces an agonizing range of sound.

The gods that sleep in the museums: the Fire God with his incense burner resembling an Inquisition tripod, Tlaloc, one of the many Water Gods with his green granite walls, the Mother Goddess of the Waters, the Mother Goddess of the Flowers, the unchanging expression echoing from beneath many layers of water of the Goddess robed in green jade, the blissful, enrapt expression, features crackling with incense, where atoms of sunlight circle around the Mother Goddess of the Flowers. This world of obligatory servitude where stone comes to life because it has been properly carved, a world of organically civilized men – I mean those whose vital organs also awaken – this human world enters into us, we participate in the dance of the gods without turning round or looking back under penalty of becoming, like ourselves, crumbling figures of salt.

In Mexico, so long as we are talking about Mexico, there is no art and things are used. And the people are continually exalted.

Unlike our idea of art, which is inert and disinterested, a genuine culture conceives of art as something magical and violently egoistical, that is, self-interested. For the Mexicans collect the *Manas*, the powers lying dormant in all forms, which cannot be released by meditation on forms for their own sake, but only arise from a magical identity with these forms. And the ancient Totems exist to stimulate the communication.

It is difficult, when everything impels us to fall into a sleep, during which we look about us with fixed, attentive eyes, to wake up and to look about as though in a dream, with eyes that no longer know what use they are and whose gaze is turned inwards.

This is how our strange idea of a disinterested action came into being, tough and active nonetheless, the more violent for having skirted around the temptation to rest.

All true effigies have a double, a shadowed self. And art fails the moment a sculptor believes that as he models he liberates a kind of shadow whose existence will unsettle him.

Like all magic cultures displayed in appropriate hieroglyphics, true theatre has its own shadows. Furthermore, of all languages and all arts, it is the only one whose shadows have shattered their limitations. From the first, we might say its shadows would not tolerate limitations.

Our fossilized idea of theatre is tied in with our fossilized idea of a shadowless culture where, whatever way we turn, our minds meet nothing but emptiness while space is full.

But true theatre, because it moves and makes use of living instruments, goes on stirring up shadows, while life endlessly stumbles along. An actor does not repeat the same gestures twice, but he gesticulates, moves and, although he brutalizes forms, as he destroys them he is united with what lives on behind and after them, producing their continuation.

Theatre, which is nothing, but uses all languages (gestures, words, sound, fire and screams), is to be found precisely at the point where the mind needs a language to bring about its manifestations.

And confining theatre to one language, speech, written words, music, lighting or sound, heralds its imminent ruin, since choosing one single language proves the inclinations we have for the facilities of that language. But one effect of a single language's limitations is that it dries up.

For theatre, just as for culture, the problem remains to designate and direct shadows. And theatre, not confined to any fixed language or form, destroys false shadows because of this, and prepares the way for another shadowed birth, uniting the true spectacle of life around it.

To shatter language in order to contact life means creating or recreating theatre. The crucial thing is not to believe this action must remain sacred, that is to say, set apart. And the main thing is to believe not that anyone can do it but that one needs to prepare for it.

This leads us to reject man's usual limitations and powers and infinitely extends the frontiers of what we call reality.

We must believe in life's meaning renewed by theatre, where man fearlessly makes himself master of the unborn, gives birth to it. And everything unborn can still be brought to life, provided we are not satisfied with remaining simple recording instruments.

Moreover, when we say the word *life*, we understand this is not life recognized by externals, by facts, but the kind of frail moving source forms never attain. And if there is one truly infernal and damned thing left today, it is our artistic dallying with forms, instead of being like those tortured at the stake, signalling through the flames.

Theatre and the Plague*

I N THE ARCHIVES OF THE SMALL TOWN of Cagliari, Sardinia, lies an account of an astonishing historic occurrence.

One night, about the end of April or the beginning of May 1720, some twenty days before the ship *Grand-Saint-Antoine* reached Marseille, where its landing coincided with the most wondrous outbreak of plague to be recorded in that city's history, Saint-Rémy, the Sardinian Viceroy, perhaps rendered more sensitive to that most baleful virus by his restricted monarchical duties, had a particularly agonizing dream. He saw himself plague-ridden and saw the disease ravage his tiny state.

Society's barriers became fluid with the effects of the scourge. Order disappeared. He witnessed the subversion of all morality, a total psychological breakdown, heard his lacerated, utterly routed bodily fluids murmur within him in a giddy wasting-away of matter, growing heavy and then gradually being transformed into carbon. Was it too late to ward off the scourge? Although organically destroyed, crushed, extirpated, his very bones consumed, he knew one does not die in dreams, that our will-power even operates *ad absurdum*, even denying what is possible, in a kind of metamorphosis of lies reborn as truth.

He awoke. He would show himself able to drive away these plague rumours and the miasmas of the oriental virus.

The *Grand-Saint-Antoine*, a month out of Beirut, requested permission to enter the harbour and dock there. At this point the Viceroy gave an insane order, an order thought raving mad, absurd, stupid and despotic both by his subjects and his suite. He hastily dispatched a pilot's boat and men to the supposedly infected vessel with orders for the *Grand-Saint-Antoine* to tack about that instant and make full sail away from the town or be sunk by cannon shot. War on the plague. The autocrat did not do things by halves.

In passing, we ought to note the unusually influential power the dream exerted on him, since it allowed him to insist on the savage

9

fierceness of his orders despite the gibes of the populace and the scepticism of his suite, when to do so meant riding roughshod not only over human rights, but even over the most ordinary respect for life, over all kinds of national and international conventions, which in the face of death no longer apply.

Be that as it may, the ship held her course, made land at Leghorn and sailed into Marseille harbour where she was allowed to dock.

The Marseille authorities have kept no record of what happened to her plague-infected cargo. We roughly know what happened to the members of her crew: they did not all die of the plague, but were scattered over various countries.

The *Grand-Saint-Antoine* did not bring the plague to Marseille, it was already there, at a particular stage of renewed activity, but its centres had been successfully localized.

The plague brought by the *Grand-Saint-Antoine* was the original, oriental virus, hence the unusually horrible aspect, the widespread flaring-up of the epidemic, which dates from its arrival and dispersion throughout the town.

This prompts a few thoughts.

This plague, which apparently revived a virus, was able to wreak a great havoc on its own, the Captain being the only member of the ship's crew who did not catch the plague. Furthermore, it did not seem that the newly arrived infected men had ever been in direct contact with those others confined to their quarantine districts. The *Grand-Saint-Antoine* passed within hailing distance of Cagliari, Sardinia, but did not leave the plague there, yet the Viceroy picked up certain of its emanations in his dreams. For one cannot deny that a substantial though subtle communication was established between the plague and himself. It is too easy to lay the blame for communication of such a disease on infection by contact alone.

But this communication between Saint-Rémy and the plague, though of sufficient intensity to release imagery in his dreams, was after all not powerful enough to infect him with the disease.

Nevertheless, the town of Cagliari, learning some time later that the ship driven from its shores by the miraculously enlightened though despotic Prince's will was the cause of the great Marseille epidemic, recorded the fact in its archives, where anyone may find it.

The 1720 Marseille plague has given us what may pass as the only clinical description we have of the scourge.

But one wonders whether the plague described by Marseille doctors was exactly the same as the 1347 Florence epidemic which produced the *Decameron*. Histories and holy books, the Bible among them, certain old medical treatises, describe the outward symptoms of all kinds of plagues whose malignant features seem to have impressed them far less than the demoralizing and prodigious effect they produced in their minds. No doubt they were right, for medicine would be hard put to establish any basic difference between the virus Pericles died of before Syracuse (if the word virus is anything more than a verbal convenience) and that appearing in the plague described by Hippocrates, which, as recent medical treatises inform us, is a kind of fictitious plague. These same treatises hold that the only genuine plague comes from Egypt, arising from the cemeteries uncovered by the subsiding Nile. The Bible and Herodotus both call attention to the lightning appearance of a plague that decimated 180,000 men of the Assyrian army in one night, thereby saving the Egyptian Empire. If this fact is true, we ought to consider the scourge as the immediate medium or materialization of a thinking power in close contact with what we call fate.

This, with or without the army of rats that hurled itself on the Assyrian troops that night, and gnawed away their accoutrements in a few hours. The above event ought to be compared with the epidemic that broke out in 660 BC in the Holy City of Mekao, Japan, on the occasion of a mere change of government.

The 1502 Provence plague, which gave Nostradamus his first opportunity to practise his powers of healing, also coincided with the most profound political upheavals, the downfall or death of kings, the disappearance and destruction of whole provinces, earthquakes, all kinds of magnetic phenomena, exodus of the Jews, preceding or following on disasters or havoc of a political or cosmic order, those causing them being too idiotic to foresee them, or not really depraved enough to desire their after-effects.

However mistaken historians or doctors may have been about the plague, I think one might agree on the idea of the disease as a kind of psychic entity, not carried by a virus. If we were to analyse closely all the facts on contagious plagues given in history or contained in archives, we would have difficulty in singling out one properly established occurrence of contagious contact, and the example Boccaccio cites of swine that died because they sniffed at sheets in which the plague-ridden had been wrapped scarcely suggests more than a kind of strange affinity between swine flesh and the nature of the plague, something which would have to be gone into very thoroughly.

Since the concept of a truly morbid entity does not exist, there are forms the mind can provisionally agree on to designate certain phenomena, and it seems our minds might agree on a plague described in the following manner.

Before any pronounced physical or psychological sickness appears, red spots appear all over the body, the sick person only suddenly noticing them when they turn black. He has no time to be alarmed by them before his head feels on fire, grows overwhelmingly heavy and he collapses. Then he is seized with terrible fatigue, a focal, magnetic, exhausting tiredness, his molecules are split in two and drawn towards their annihilation. His fluids, wildly jumbled in disorder, seem to race through his body. His stomach heaves, his insides seem to want to burst out between his teeth. His pulse sometimes slows down until it becomes a shadow, a latent pulse; at other times it races in accordance with his seething inner fever, the streaming wanderings of his mind. His pulse beating as fast as his heart, growing intense, heavy, deafening; those eyes, first inflamed, then glazed. That hugely swollen panting tongue, first white, then red, then black, as if charred and cracked, all heralding unprecedented organic disturbances. Soon the fluids, furrowed like the earth by lightning, like a volcano tormented by subterranean upheavals, seek an outlet. Fiery cones are formed at the centre of each spot and around them the skin rises up in blisters like air bubbles under a skin of lava. These blisters are surrounded by rings, the outer one, just like Saturn's ring at maximum radiance, indicating the outer edge of the bubo.

The body is streaked with them. Just as volcanoes have their own chosen locations on earth, the buboes have their own chosen spots over the expanse of the human body. Buboes appear around the anus, under the armpits, at those precious places where the active glands steadily carry out their functions, and through these buboes the anatomy discharges either its inner putrefaction, or in other cases, life itself. A violent burning sensation localized in one spot more often than not indicates that the life force has lost none of its strength and that abatement of the sickness or even a cure may be possible. Like silent rage, the most terrible plague is one that does not disclose its symptoms.

Once open, a plague victim's body exhibits no lesions. The gall bladder, which filters heavier, solid organic waste, is full, swollen to bursting point with a sticky black liquid, so dense it suggests new matter. Arterial and venial blood is also black and sticky. The body is as hard as stone. On the walls of the stomach membrane countless blood sources have arisen and everything points to a basic disorder in secretion. But there is neither loss nor destruction as in leprosy or syphilis. The intestines themselves, the site of the bloodiest disorders, where matter reaches an unbelievable degree of decomposition and calcification, are not organically affected. The gall bladder, from which the hardest matter must be virtually torn as in some human sacrifices, with a sharp knife, an obsidian instrument, hard and glazed – the gall bladder is hypertrophied and fragile in places, yet intact, without an iota missing, any visible lesions or loss of matter.

However, in some cases, the lesioned brain and lungs blacken and become gangrenous. The softened, chopped-up lungs fall in chips of an unknown black substance; the brain, fissured, crushed and disintegrated, is reduced to powder, to a kind of coal-black dust.*

Two notable observations can be made about the above facts. The first is that the plague syndrome is complete without any gangrene in the lungs or brain and the plague victim dies without any putrefaction in his limbs. Without underestimating the disease, the anatomy does not need localized physical gangrene to decide to die.

Secondly one notes that the only two organs really affected and injured by the plague, the brain and lungs, are both dependent on consciousness or the will. We can stop breathing or thinking, speed up our breath, induce any rhythm we choose, make it conscious or unconscious at will, bring about a balance between both kinds of breathing; automatic, under direct control of the sympathetic nerve, and the other, which obeys each new conscious mental reflex.

We can also speed up, slow down or accent our thoughts. We can regulate the subconscious interplay of the mind. We cannot control the filtering of the fluids by the liver, the redistribution of the blood within the anatomy by the heart and arteries, control digestion, stop or speed up the elimination of substances in the intestines. Hence the plague seems to make its presence known in those places, to have a liking for all those physical localities where human will-power, consciousness and thought are at hand or in a position to occur.

During the 1880s, a French doctor called Yersin, working on the corpses of Indo-Chinese who had died of the plague, isolated one of these round-headed, short-tailed bacilli only visible under a microscope, and called it the plague microbe. In my eyes, this is only a much smaller, infinitely smaller material factor, which appears at any moment during the development of the virus, but does not help to explain the plague at all. And I would rather this doctor had told me why all great plagues last five months, with or without a virus, after which the virulence dies down, and how the Turkish Ambassador, passing through Languedoc towards the end of 1720, could draw an imaginary line from Nice to Bordeaux passing through Avignon and Toulouse, as the outer geographic limit of the scourge's spread, events proving him correct.

From the above it is apparent that the disease has an inner nature whose laws cannot be scientifically specified and it would be useless to try and fix its geographic source, since the Egyptian plague is not the oriental plague, which is not Hippocrates's, which is not the Syracusan, which is not the Florentine (the Black Death) which accounted for fifty million lives in medieval Europe. No one can say why the plague strikes a fleeing coward and spares a rake taking his pleasure with the corpses of the dead. Why isolation, chastity or solitude are ineffectual against the scourge's attacks, or why a group of debauchees who have retired to the countryside – as did Boccaccio, his two well-equipped companions and their seven lustful devotees – could calmly await the hot weather when the plague subsides. Or why in a nearby castle, turned into a warlike fortress ringed with troops barring anyone from entering, the plague turned the garrison and all the occupants into corpses, yet spared the guards, alone exposed to infection. Equally, who could explain why the sanitary cordons set up with great numbers of troops by Mehmet Ali, about the end of the last century at the time of a fresh outbreak of Egyptian plague, effectively protected convents, schools, prisons and palaces. Or why many outbreaks of the plague which had all the characteristics of the oriental plague could suddenly have broken out in medieval Europe in places without any contact with the East.

Out of these peculiarities, mysteries, contradictions and traits, we ought to be able to construct the inner nature of a disease which saps the anatomy and life, until it is torn apart and causes spasms, like pain which, as it intensifies, strikes deeper, increases its resources and means of access in every ramification of our sensibility.

But out of the mental freedom with which the plague evolves, without any rats, germs or contact, we can deduce the dark, ultimate action of a spectacle I am going to try and analyse.

Once the plague is established in a city, normal social order collapses. There is no more refuse collection, no more army, police or municipality. Pyres are lit to burn the dead whenever men are available. Each family wants its own. Then wood, space and fire grow scarce, families fight around the pyres, soon to be followed by general flight since there are too many corpses. The streets are already choked with crumbling pyramids of the dead, the vermin gnawing at the edges. The stench rises in the air like tongues of flame. Whole streets are blocked by mounds of dead. Then the houses are thrown open and raving plague victims disperse through the streets howling, their minds full of horrible visions. The disease gnawing at their vitals, running through their whole anatomy, is discharged in mental outbursts. Other plague victims, lacking buboes or delirium, pain or rashes, examine themselves proudly in the mirror, feeling in splendid health, only to fall dead with their shaving dishes in their hands, full of scorn for other victims.

Over the thick, bloody, noxious streaming gutters, the colour of anguish and opium, spurting from the corpses, strange men clothed in wax, with noses an ell long and glass eyes, mounted on kinds of Japanese sandals made up of a double arrangement of wooden slabs, a horizontal one in the form of a sole, with the uprights isolating them from the infected liquids, pass by chanting absurd litanies, though their sanctity does not prevent them falling into the holocaust in turn. These ignorant doctors only show their fear and childishness.

The scum of the populace, immunized so it seems by their frantic greed, enter the open houses and help themselves to riches they know will serve no purpose or profit. At this point, theatre establishes itself. Theatre, that is to say, the sense of gratuitous urgency with which they are driven to perform useless acts of no present advantage.

The remaining survivors go berserk; the virtuous and obedient son kills his father, the continent sodomize their kin. The lewd become chaste. The miser chucks handfuls of his gold out of the windows, the soldier hero sets fire to the town he had formerly risked his life to save. Dandies deck themselves out and stroll among the charnel houses. Neither the lack of sanctions nor the imminence of death are enough to explain such pointlessly absurd acts by people who did not believe death could end anything. And how are we to explain that upsurge of erotic fever among the recovered victims who, instead of escaping, stay behind, seeking out and snatching sinful pleasure from the dying or even the dead, half-crushed under the pile of corpses where chance had lodged them?

But if a major scourge is needed to make this frenzied pointlessness appear and if that scourge is called the plague, we might perhaps attempt to determine the value of this pointlessness in relation to our whole personality. The condition of a plague victim who dies without any material destruction, yet with all the stigmata of an absolute, almost abstract disease upon him, is in the same condition as an actor totally penetrated by feelings without any benefit or relation to reality. Everything in the actor's physical aspect, just as in the plague victim, shows life has reacted to a paroxysm, yet nothing has happened.

Between the shrieking plague-ridden who run in pursuit of their imaginings, and actors in pursuit of their sensibility, between a living man who invents characters he would never have thought of dreaming up without the plague, bringing them to life amidst an audience of corpses and raving lunatics, and the poet who inopportunely invents characters entrusting them to an equally inert or delirious audience, there are other analogies which account for the only important truths, placing theatre action, like that of the plague, on a par with a true epidemic.

Whereas plague imagery related to an advanced state of physical disorganization is like the last outbursts of waning mental strength, the imagery of poetry in the theatre is a mental power which, beginning its trajectory in the tangible, dispenses with reality. Once launched in fury, an actor needs infinitely more virtue to stop himself committing a crime than a murderer needs to perpetrate his crime, and this is where, in their pointlessness, these acts of stage feeling appear as something infinitely more valid than those feelings worked out in life.

Compared with a murderer's fury that exhausts itself, an actor of tragedy remains enclosed within a circle. The murderer's anger has accomplished an act and is released, losing contact with the power that inspired but will no longer sustain it. It has assumed a form, while the actor's fury, which denies itself by being detached, is rooted in the universal.

If we are now prepared to accept this mental picture of the plague, we can consider the plague victim's disturbed fluids as a solidified, substantial aspect of a disorder which on other levels is equivalent to the clashes, struggles, disasters and devastation brought about by events. Just as it is not impossible that the unconsumed despair of a lunatic screaming in an asylum can cause the plague, so by a kind of reversibility of feelings and imagery, in the same way we can admit that outward events, political conflicts, natural disasters, revolutionary order and wartime chaos, when they occur on a theatre level, are released into the audience's sensitivity with the strength of an epidemic.

In *The City of God*, St Augustine points to the similarity of the plague, which kills without destroying any organs, and theatre, which, without killing, induces the most mysterious changes not only in the minds of individuals but in a whole nation.

"Know then," he writes, "you who are ignorant of this, that these plays, exhibitions of shameless folly and licence, were established at Rome not by the vicious craving of men but by the appointment of your gods. Much more pardonably might you have rendered divine honours to Scipio* than to gods such as these; indeed, the gods were not so moral as their pontiff!...

"They enjoined that plays be exhibited in their honour to stay a physical pestilence, while their pontiff prohibited the theatre to prevent a moral pestilence. If then there remains in you sufficient mental enlightenment to prefer the soul to the body, choose whom you will worship. But these astute and wicked spirits, foreseeing that in due course the pestilence would shortly cease, took occasion to infect, not the bodies, but the morals of their worshippers, with a far more serious disease. And in this plague these gods found great enjoyment because it benighted the minds of men with so gross a darkness and dishonoured them with so foul a deformity that even quite recently some of those who fled from the sack of Rome and found refuge in Carthage were so infected with the disease that day after day they seemed to contend with one another who should most madly run after the actors in the theatre."

There is no point in trying to give exact reasons for this infectious madness. It would be as much use trying to find reasons why the nervous system after a certain time is in tune with the vibrations of the subtlest music and is eventually somehow lastingly modified by it. Above all we must agree stage acting is a delirium like the plague, and is communicable.

The mind believes what it sees and does what it believes; that is the secret of fascination. And in his book, St Augustine does not doubt the reality of this fascination for one moment.

Yet conditions must be found to give birth to a spectacle that can fascinate the mind. It is not just a matter of art.

For if theatre is like the plague, this is not just because it acts on large groups and disturbs them in one and the same way. There is both something victorious and vengeful in theatre just as in the plague, for we clearly feel that the spontaneous fire the plague lights as it passes by is nothing but a gigantic liquidation.

Such a complete social disaster, such organic disorder overflowing with vice, this kind of wholesale exorcism constricting the soul, driving it to the limit, indicates the presence of a condition which is an extreme force and where all the powers of nature are newly rediscovered the instant something fundamental is about to be accomplished.

The plague takes dormant images, latent disorder and suddenly carries them to the point of the most extreme gestures. Theatre also takes gestures and develops them to the limit. Just like the plague, it reforges the links between what does and does not exist, between the virtual nature of the possible and the material nature of existence. It rediscovers the idea of figures and archetypal symbols which act like sudden silences, fermatas, heart stops, adrenalin calls, incendiary images surging into our abruptly woken minds. It restores all our dormant conflicts and their powers, giving these powers names we acknowledge as signs. Here a bitter clash of symbols takes place before us, hurled one against the other in an inconceivable riot. For theatre can only happen the moment the inconceivable really begins, where poetry taking place on stage nourishes and superheats created symbols.

These symbols are symbols of full-blown powers held in bondage until that moment and unusable in real life, exploding in the guise of incredible images giving existence and the freedom of the city to acts naturally opposed to social life.

A real stage play disturbs our peace of mind, releases our repressed subconscious, drives us to a kind of potential rebellion (since it retains its full value only if it remains potential), calling for a difficult heroic attitude on the part of the assembled groups.

As soon as the curtain goes up on Ford's *'Tis Pity She's a Whore*, to our great surprise we see before us a man launched on a most arrogant defence of incest, exerting all his youthful, conscious strength both in proclaiming and justifying it.

He does not hesitate or waver for one instant, thereby demonstrating just how little all the barriers mean that might be set up against him. He is heroically guilty, boldly, openly heroic. Everything drives him in this direction, inflames him, there is no heaven and no earth for him, only the strength of his tumultuous passion, which evokes a correspondingly rebellious and heroic passion in Annabella.

"I weep," she says, "not with remorse, but for fear I shall not be able to satisfy my passion." They are both falsifiers, hypocrites and liars for the sake of their superhuman passion, obstructed, persecuted by the law, but which they place above the law.

Revenge for revenge, crime for crime. While we believed them threatened, hunted, lost and we were ready to feel pity for them as victims, they show themselves ready to trade blow for blow with fate and threat for threat.

We follow them from one demand to the other, from one excess to the next. Annabella is caught, convicted of adultery and incest, she is trampled upon, insulted, dragged along by the hair but, to our great astonishment, instead of trying to make excuses she provokes her executioner even more and sings out in a kind of stubborn heroism. This is final rebellion, exemplary love without respite, making the audience gasp with anxiety in case anything should ever end it.

If one is looking for an example of total freedom in rebellion, Ford's *'Tis Pity* offers us this poetic example coupled with a picture of ultimate danger.

And just when we think we have reached a climax of horror and bloodshed, of flaunted laws, in short, poetry consecrating rebellion, we are obliged to continue in a vortex nothing can stop.

At the end we tell ourselves there must be retribution and death for such boldness and for such an irresistible crime.

Yet it is not so. Giovanni, the lover, inspired by a great impassioned poet, places himself above retribution and crime by a kind of indescribably passionate crime, places himself above threats, above horror by an even greater horror that baffles both law and morals and those who dare to set themselves up as judges.

A clever trap is laid; orders are given for a great banquet where henchmen and hired assassins hide among the guests, ready to pounce on him at the first sign. But this lost, hunted hero inspired by love will not allow anyone to judge that love.

He seems to say, you want my love's flesh and blood, but I mean to hurl it in your face, I intend to splatter you with the blood of a love whose level you could never attain.

So he kills his beloved and rips out her heart as if to eat his fill of it in the midst of that feast where the guests had hoped perhaps to devour him themselves.

He kills his rival before his execution, his sister's husband who had dared to come between himself and his mistress, slaying him in a final duel which then appears to be his own death throes.

Like the plague, theatre is a powerful appeal through illustration to those powers which return the mind to the origins of its inner struggles. And we clearly sense Ford's passionate example is only a symbol for a much greater and absolutely fundamental task.

The terrifying apparition of Evil produced in unalloyed form at the Eleusinian Mysteries being truly revealed corresponded to the darker moments in certain ancient tragedies which all theatre must rediscover.

If fundamental theatre is like the plague, this is not because it is contagious, but because like the plague it is a revelation, urging forwards the exteriorization of a latent undercurrent of cruelty through which all the perversity of which the mind is capable, whether in a person or a nation, becomes localized.

Just like the plague it is a time for evil, the victory of dark powers, a higher power nourishing them until they have died out.

In theatre, as in the plague, there is a kind of strange sun, an unusually bright light by which the difficult, even the impossible, suddenly appears to be our natural medium. And Ford's 'Tis Pity She's a Whore is lit by the brilliance of that strange sun just as is all worthwhile theatre. It resembles the plague's freedom where, step by step, stage by stage, the victim's character swells out, where the survivors gradually become imposing, superhuman beings.

Now one may say all true freedom is dark, infallibly identified with sexual freedom, also dark, without knowing exactly why. For the Platonic Eros, the reproductive impulse, the freedom of life, disappeared long ago beneath the turbid surface of the *Libido* which we associate with everything sullied, despicable and ignominious in the fact of living, the headlong rush with our customary, impure vitality, with constantly renewed strength, in the direction of life.

Thus all great Myths are dark and one cannot imagine all the great Fables aside from a mood of slaughter, torture and bloodshed, telling the masses about the original division of the sexes and the slaughter of essences that came with creation.

Theatre, like the plague, is made in the image of this slaughter, this essential division. It unravels conflicts, liberates powers, releases potential and if these and the powers are dark, this is not the fault of the plague or theatre, but life.

We do not see that life as it stands and as it has been made offers us much cause for exaltation. It seems as though a colossal abscess, ethical as much as social, is drained by the plague. And like the plague, theatre is collectively made to drain abscesses.

It may be true that the poison of theatre, when injected into the body of society, destroys it, as St Augustine asserted, but it does so as a plague, a revenging scourge, a redeeming epidemic when credulous ages were convinced they saw God's hand in it, while it was nothing more than a natural law applied, where all gestures were offset by another gesture, every action by a reaction.

Like the plague, theatre is a crisis resolved either by death or cure. The plague is a superior disease because it is an absolute crisis after which there is nothing left except death or drastic purification. In the same way, theatre is a disease because it is a final balance that cannot be obtained without destruction. It urges the mind on to delirium which intensifies its energy. And finally from a human viewpoint we can see that the effect of the theatre is as beneficial as the plague, impelling us to see ourselves as we are, making the masks fall and divulging our world's lies, aimlessness, meanness and even two-facedness. It shakes off stifling material dullness which even overcomes the senses' clearest testimony, and collectively reveals their dark powers and hidden strength to men, urging them to take a nobler, more heroic stand in the face of destiny than they would have assumed without it.

And the question we must now ask ourselves is to know whether in this world that is slipping away, committing suicide without realizing it, a nucleus of men can be found to impress this higher idea of theatre on the world, to bring to all of us a natural, occult equivalent of the dogma we no longer believe.

Production and Metaphysics*

There is a work by a Primitive painter in the Louvre, whether known or unknown I cannot say, who will never represent a major school in art history. The artist's name is Lucas van Leyden* and to my mind he invalidates the four or five hundred years of painting coming after him, rendering them useless. The painting in question is entitled *Lot and His Daughters*, a biblical subject in the style of the period. The Middle Ages certainly did not interpret the Bible as we do today and this painting is a strange example of the mystical inferences which can be deduced from it. In any event, its pathos is noticeable even from a distance,* since it affects the mind by a kind of striking visual harmony, intensely active in the whole work yet caught at a glance. Even before we have made out the subject, we get the feeling something important is happening and it seems the ear is as affected by it as the eye. A tremendously important mental drama appears accumulated there, like a sudden cloud formation which the wind or some more immediate fate has blown there to assess their thunderbolts.

And, in fact, in the painting the sky is dark and overcast, but even before we can make out that this drama originated in the heavens, took place in the heavens, the strange colouring and jumble of forms, the impression emanating from it at a distance, all foretells a kind of natural drama, and I defy any other artist of the Golden Ages to offer us anything like it.

A tent is pitched on the shore, in front of which Lot is seated, wearing a breastplate and sporting a fine red beard, watching his daughters parade before him as if he were a guest at a prostitutes' banquet.

And in fact they strut about, some mothers, others Amazons, combing their hair or fencing, as if they had never had any other object than to please their father, to serve as his creatures or playthings. Here we see the deeply incestuous nature of this old subject which the artist has developed in sexual imagery, a proof that he has fully understood all its deep sexuality in a modern way, that is to say as we would understand it ourselves. A proof that its deeply sexual but poetic nature did not escape him any more than it did us.

23

On the left of the painting, slightly in the background, a black tower rises to fantastic heights, its base supported by a network of rocks and plants, twisting roads marked by milestones, with houses dotted here and there. And by an apt perspective effect, one of these paths which had been threading its way through the maze stands out at a given spot, crosses a bridge, is finally caught in a shaft of that stormy light spilling out between the clouds, in which the region is fitfully bathed. In the background, the sea is very high besides being extraordinarily calm, considering the fiery web seething in one corner of the sky.

Sometimes, when we are watching exploding fireworks, some details of the landscape stand out against the darkness in the ghostly light, in the nocturnal gunfire of shooting stars, sky rockets and Roman candles; trees, tower, mountains and houses appear in relief before our eyes, their colour and appearance for ever remaining associated in our minds with a notion of ear-splitting noise. There is no better way of conveying how the various aspects of the landscape conform to this fire revealed in the sky than by saying that although they possess their own colour, in spite of everything, they remain related to it like muted echoes, like living points of reference born within it, put there to allow it to exert its full destructive power.

Besides, there is something horribly forceful and disturbing about the way the painter depicts this fire, like active, changing features in a set expression. It makes little difference how this effect is achieved, it is real. One has only to see the painting to be convinced of it.

In any case, this fire, which no one will deny gives one the impression of an evil intellect emanating from it, by its very violence mentally serves to counterbalance the heavy material solidity of the remainder.

To the right, on the same perspective level as the black tower, a narrow spit of land surrounded by a ruined monastery juts out between the heavens and high seas.

This spit of land, however near it may appear to the shore where Lot's tent is pitched, still leaves room for a vast gulf where an unprecedented maritime disaster seems to have taken place. Ships broken in two but not yet sunk are propped up on the sea as if on crutches, while the water round about them is full of their uprooted masts and broken spars.

It is hard to say why such an impression of absolute disaster emanates from the sight of one or two shipwrecked vessels.

It seems as though the painter knew certain secrets about linear proportion and how to make it affect the mind directly like a physical reagent. In any case this impression of intellect spread abroad in outdoor nature, especially the manner of portraying it, is apparent in several other details on the canvas, such as the bridge standing out against the sea, high as an eight-storey house,* with people filing across it, like Ideas in Plato's cave.

It would be untrue to claim that the thoughts emerging from this painting are clear. At all events they are of a grandeur to which we have become totally unaccustomed during the last few centuries by painting that was merely painting.

In addition, Lot and his daughters suggest an idea of sexuality and reproduction, and Lot seems placed there like a drone, to take improper advantage of his daughters.

This is almost the only social idea in the picture.

All the other ideas are metaphysical. I am sorry to have to use that word, but that is what they are called. And I might even say their poetic greatness, their tangible effect on us arises from the fact that they are metaphysical, that their mental profundity cannot be separated from the painting's formal, external symmetry.

Furthermore there is an idea of change in the different landscape details and the way they are painted, their levels annulling or corresponding to one another, that leads us into the mind in painting the same way as in music.

There is another idea about Fate, revealed not so much by the appearance of that sudden fire as by the solemn way in which all forms are arranged or disarranged beneath it, some as if bent beneath a gust of irresistible panic, the others motionless, almost ironic, all obeying a powerful intelligent consistency, seemingly nature's mind externalized.

There are also ideas on Chaos, the Marvellous and Balance. There are even one or two on the impotence of Words, this supremely anarchic, material painting seeming to establish their futility.

In any event I must say this painting is what theatre ought to be, if only it knew how to speak its own language.

And I ask this question:

How can it be that in the theatre, at least theatre such as we know it in Europe, or rather in the West, everything specifically theatrical, that is to say, everything which cannot be expressed in words or, if you prefer, everything that is not contained in dialogue (dialogue itself viewed as a function of sound amplification on stage and the *requirements* of that sound) has been left in the background?

Besides, how can it be that Western theatre (I say Western theatre as luckily there are others such as oriental theatre, which have known how to keep theatrical concepts intact, whereas in the West this idea – just like all others – has been *debased*), how is it Western theatre cannot conceive of theatre under any other aspect than dialogue form?

Dialogue – something written and spoken – does not specifically belong to the stage but to books. The proof is that there is a special section in literary history textbooks on drama as a subordinate branch in the history of spoken language.

I maintain the stage is a tangible, physical place that needs to be filled and it ought to be allowed to speak its own concrete language.

I maintain that this physical language, aimed at the senses and independent of speech, must first satisfy the senses. There must be poetry for the senses just as there is for speech, but this physical, tangible language I am referring to is really only theatrical insofar as the thoughts it expresses escape spoken language.

You might ask what these thoughts are that words cannot express, and which would find a more fitting, ideal expression than words in a physical, tangible stage language?

I will answer this question later.

The most urgent thing seems to me to decide what this physical language is composed of, this solid, material language by which theatre can be distinguished from words.

It is composed of everything filling the stage, everything that can be shown and materially expressed on stage, intended first of all to appeal to the senses, instead of being addressed primarily to the mind, like spoken language. (I am well aware words also have their own sound potential, different ways of being projected into space, called *inflection*. Besides, one could say a great deal about the tangible value of inflections in theatre, about the power of words to create their own music according to the way they are pronounced, distinct from their actual meaning and even running counter to that meaning – to create an undercurrent of impressions, connections and affinities beneath language. But this theatrical way of looking at language is already a subordinate *aspect* to the dramatist and one to which he no longer pays attention, especially today, in creating his plays. Well, let it go at that.)

This language created for the senses must first take care to satisfy the senses. This would not prevent it later amplifying its full mental effect on all possible levels and along all lines. It would also permit spatial poetry to take the place of language poetry and to be resolved in the exact field of whatever does not properly apply to words.

In order to understand what I have said better, doubtless a few examples of this spatial poetry would be desirable, able as it is to give birth to those kinds of substantial imagery, the equivalent of word imagery. Examples will be found below.

This difficult, complex poetry assumes many guises: first of all it assumes those expressive means usable on stage* such as music, dance, plastic arts, mimicry, mime, gesture, voice inflection, architecture, lighting and decor.

Each of these means has its own specific poetry as well as a kind of ironic poetry arising from the way it combines with other expressive means. It is easy to see the result of these combinations, their interaction and mutual subversion.

I will return below to the subject of this poetry which can only be fully effective if it is tangible, that is to say if it objectively produces something owing to its *active* presence on stage – if, as in the Balinese theatre, a sound corresponds to a certain gesture and instead of acting as decor accompanying thought, makes it develop, guiding it, destroying it or decisively changing it, etc.

One form of this spatial poetry – beyond any brought about by an arrangement of lines, forms, colours and objects in their natural state, such as are found in all the arts – belongs to sign language. And I hope I may mention that other aspect of pure theatre language that escapes words, that sign, gesture and posture language with its own ideographic values, such as they exist in some undebased mime plays.

By "undebased mime plays" I mean straightforward mime, where gestures, instead of standing for words or sentences as in European mime (barely fifty years old) where they are merely a distortion of the silent parts in Italian comedy, stand for ideas, attitudes of mind, aspects of nature in a tangible, potent way, that is to say by always evoking natural things or details, like that oriental language which portrays night by a tree on which a bird that has already closed one eye is beginning to close the other. And another abstract idea or attitude of mind could be portrayed by some of the innumerable symbols in Scripture, such as the eye of the needle through which the camel cannot pass.

We can see these signs form true hieroglyphics where man, insofar as he contributes to making them, is only one form like any other, to which he nevertheless adds particular prestige because of his duality.

This language conjures up intense images of natural or mental poetry in the mind and gives us a good idea of what spatial poetry, if free from spoken language, could become in the theatre.

Whatever the position of this language and poetry may be,* I have noticed that in our theatre, which exists under the exclusive dictatorship of words, this language of symbols and mimicry, this silent mime play, these attitudes and spatial gestures, this objective inflection, in short everything I look on as specifically theatrical in the theatre, all these elements when they exist outside the script are generally considered the lowest part of theatre, are casually called "craft" and are associated with what is known as staging or "production". We are lucky when the word staging is not just tagged on to the idea of external artistic lavishness solely connected with costume, lighting and decor.

Against this viewpoint, which seems to me completely Western or rather Latin, that is, pig-headed, I might even say that inasmuch as this language starts on stage, drawing its effectiveness from its spontaneous creation on stage, inasmuch as it exerts itself directly on stage without passing through words (and why could we not envisage a play composed right on stage, produced on stage) – staging is theatre far more than a written, spoken play. No doubt I will be asked what is specifically Latin about this view which is opposed to mime. What is Latin is the need to use words to express obvious ideas. For me obvious ideas, in theatre as in all else, are dead and finished.

The idea of a play built right on stage, encountering production and performance obstacles, demands the discovery of active language, both active and anarchic, where the usual limits of feelings and words are transcended.

In any event, and I hasten to say so at once, theatre which submits staging and production, that is to say everything about it that is specifically theatrical, to the lines, is mad, crazy, perverted, rhetorical, philistine, anti-poetic and positivist – that is to say, Western theatre.

Furthermore, I am well aware that a language of gestures and postures, dance and music is less able to define a character, to narrate man's thoughts, to explain conscious states clearly and exactly, than spoken language. But whoever said theatre was made to define a character, to resolve conflicts of a human, emotional order, of a present-day psychological nature such as those which monopolize current theatre?

Given theatre as we see it here, one would imagine there was nothing more to know than whether we will have a good fuck, whether we will go to war or be cowardly enough to sue for peace, how we will put up with our petty moral anxieties, whether we will become conscious of our "complexes" (in scientific language) or whether our "complexes" will silence us. Moreover, rarely does the debate rise to a social level or do we question our social or ethical system. Our theatre never goes so far as to ask itself whether by chance this social or ethical system is iniquitous or not.

Now to my mind the present state of society is iniquitous and ought to be destroyed. If it is theatre's role to be concerned with it, it is even more a matter for machine guns. Our theatre is not even able to ask this question in as effective and incendiary a manner as is needed, and even if it did ask it, it would still be far from its intended purpose, which is higher and even more mysterious.

All the topics detailed above stink of mankind, of materialistic, temporary mankind, I might even say *carrion man*. These personal worries disgust me, utterly disgust me as does just about all current theatre, which is as human as it is anti-poetic and, except for three or four plays, seems to me to stink of decadence and pus.

Current theatre is in decline because on the one hand it has lost any feeling for seriousness, and on the other for laughter. Because it has broken away from solemnity, from direct, harmful effectiveness – in a word, from Danger.

For it has lost any true sense of humour and laughter's physical, anarchic, dissolving power.

Because it has broken away from the profoundly anarchic spirit at the basis of all poetry.

One must admit that everything in the purpose of an object, the meaning or use of a natural form, is a matter of convention.

Though nature gave a tree the shape of a tree, it could just as well have given it the shape of an animal or a hill and we would have thought *tree* before animal or hill and the trick would have been played.

We all agree a beautiful woman has a pleasing voice. Yet if from when the world began we had heard all beautiful women call us by snorting through their trunks and greet us by trumpeting, we would ever after have associated the idea of trumpeting with the idea of a beautiful woman and a part of our inner vision of the world would have been radically changed.

Thus we can understand poetry is anarchic inasmuch as it questions all object relationships or those between meaning and form. It is also anarchic to the extent its occurrence is the result of disturbances leading us nearer to chaos.

I will give no further examples. One could go on for ever, not only with humorous ones such as those I have just used.

Theatrically, this inversion of forms, these altered meanings, could become the essential element of this humorous spatial poetry, staging's exclusive province.

In one of the Marx Brothers' films a man, thinking he is about to take a woman in his arms, ends up with a cow which moos. And through a combination of circumstances too long to relate, at that moment that same moo assumes an intellectual dignity equal to a woman's cry.

If such a situation is possible in films, it is no less possible in theatre as it stands, and it would take very little; for example the cow might be replaced by an animated puppet, a kind of monster gifted with speech, or a man disguised as an animal – to rediscover the secret of the objective poetry underlying all humour, which theatre has given up, leaving it for music hall, while the cinema later turned it to good account.

I mentioned danger in a preceding paragraph. Now it seems to me the best way of producing this concept of danger on stage is by the objective unforeseen, not unforeseen in situations but in things, the sudden inopportune passing from a mental image to a true image. For example a man cursing suddenly sees the image of his curse realistically materialized before him (provided, I might add, this image was not utterly pointless, but engenders in turn other imagery of the same mental spirit).

Another example would be to have a fabricated being appear, made of wood and cloth, completely invented, resembling nothing, yet of a disturbing nature, able to reintroduce on stage the slightest intimation of the great metaphysical fear underlying all ancient theatre.

The Balinese with their imaginary dragon, like all orientals, have not lost the sense of this mysterious fear, since they know it is one of the most stirring and indeed essential elements in theatre when the latter is restored to its proper level.

For whether we like it or not, true poetry is metaphysical and I might even say it is its metaphysical scope, its degree of metaphysical effectiveness, which gives it its proper value.

This is the second or third time I have mentioned metaphysics. I also mentioned dead ideas above while speaking about psychology and I expect many people will be tempted to tell me that if there is one inhuman idea on earth, one ineffective, dead idea which means very little even to the mind, it is metaphysics.

As René Guénon said, this is due "to our purely Western manner, our anti-poetic, truncated way of regarding first principles (apart from the forceful, massive state of mind corresponding to them)".

In oriental theatre with its metaphysical inclinations, as against Western theatre and its psychological inclinations, this whole complex of gestures, signs, postures and sound which make up a stage-production language, this language which develops all its physical and poetic effects on all conscious levels and in all senses, must lead to thought adopting deep attitudes which might be called *active metaphysics*.

I will return to this later. For the moment let us go back to theatre as we know it.

I attended a discussion on theatre a few days ago where I saw some of those creepy men, otherwise known as playwrights, come and explain to me how to insinuate a play into a producer's favour, like those men in history who *introduced* poison into their rival's ears. I believe the matter under discussion was settling the direction theatre must take, in other words its future destiny.

Nothing was settled and at no time was there any question of theatre's true fate, that is to say what, by nature and definition, theatre is destined to represent, nor those means at its command to do so. On the contrary, theatre seemed to me like a kind of frozen world, with players frozen in gestures that were no longer of any use to them,

31

brittle inflections overheard already falling to pieces, with music reduced to kinds of ciphers whose signs were beginning to fade, and kinds of luminous explosions, themselves solidified and corresponding to the traces of moves – and all about an incredible fluttering of men in black suits busy arguing over receipts by the entrance to a white-hot box office. As if theatre organization were henceforth reduced to everything peripheral and theatre was reduced to everything that is not theatre, while its pervading tone stinks to high heaven to people of taste.

To my mind theatre merges with production potential when the most extreme poetic results are derived from it, and theatre's production potential is wholly related to staging viewed as a language of movement in space.

Now to derive the furthest poetic consequences from means of production is to make metaphysics out of them and I do not believe anyone could argue with that way of looking at the problem.

It seems to me that to make metaphysics out of language, gestures, postures, decor and music is, from a theatrical point of view, to regard it in relation to all the ways it can have of agreeing with time and movement.

To give objective examples of the poetry resulting from the various ways gesture, sound or inflection supports itself with more or less insistence on such and such a spatial area at such and such a moment would appear to me as difficult as to communicate the feeling of the special quality of a sound in words, or the intensity and nature of physical pain. It all depends on production and can only be determined on stage.

Here and now I ought to review all the means of expression open to theatre (or staging, which, in the system I have just expanded, is merged with it). But that would entail too much and I will select only one or two examples.

First, on spoken language.

To make metaphysics out of spoken language is to make language convey what it does not normally convey. That is to use it in a new, exceptional and unusual way, to give it its full, physical shock potential, to split it up and distribute it actively in space, to treat inflections in a completely tangible manner and restore their shattering power and really to manifest something; to turn against language and its basely utilitarian, one might almost say alimentary sources, against its origins as a hunted beast, and finally to consider language in the form of *Incantation*.

This whole active, poetic way of visualizing stage expression leads us to turn away from present-day theatre's human, psychological meaning and to rediscover a religious, mystical meaning our theatre has forgotten.

Besides, if one has only to say words like *religious* and *mystic* to be taken for a sexton or a profoundly illiterate bonze only fit for rattling prayer wheels outside a Buddhist temple, this is a simple judgement on our incapacity to draw all the inferences from words and our profound ignorance of the spirit of synthesis and analogy.

It may also mean that we have reached the point where we have lost all contact with true theatre, since we restrict it to the field of whatever everyday thought can achieve, to the known or unknown field of consciousness – and if theatrically we turn to the subconscious it is merely to steal what it may have been able to collect (or hide) in the way of accessible mundane experiences.

Let it be further said that one of the reasons for the physical effectiveness on the mind, the direct, active power of the images in certain oriental theatre productions such as those of the Balinese theatre, is that theatre rests on age-old traditions, having kept the secret use of gestures, inflections and harmony intact, in relation to the senses and on all possible levels – this does not condemn oriental theatre but censures us and with us the state we live in, which must be destroyed so we may apply ourselves to eliminating it vindictively in every sphere where it hinders the free application of thought.

Alchemist Theatre*

A secret similarity exists between the fundamental principles of theatre and those of alchemy. For when one considers theatre's nature, its foundations, like alchemy it is anchored to a certain number of bases, the same for all arts, aiming in the imaginary, mental field at being as effective as that which *really* turns matter into gold in the physical field. But there is an even higher likeness between theatre and alchemy, leading us much further metaphysically. That is, alchemy and theatre are virtual arts, so to speak, and do not contain their object within them any more than they contain their reality.

Where alchemy, through its signs, is like the mental Double of an act effective on the level of real matter alone, theatre ought also to be considered as the Double not of this immediate, everyday reality which has been slowly truncated to a mere lifeless copy, as empty as it is saccharined, but another, deadlier archetypal reality in which Origins, like dolphins, quickly dive back into the gloom of the deep once they have shown their heads.

For this reality is not human but inhuman and we must admit man, his customs and nature count for little in it. Man's head might barely remain, a kind of soft, stripped, organic head in which just enough positive matter would be left for first principles to be able to exert their effects within it in a sensible, final manner.

Before going on, we ought to note the strange proclivity all books dealing with alchemy maintain for theatre terms, as if their authors had from the start felt everything *productive*, that is to say everything theatrical, in the whole series of *symbols* by which the Great Work occurs mentally, while waiting for it to occur substantially in real life, as well as in the digressions of an uninformed mind, of all the acts and in what one might term the "dialectic" sequence of all the wanderings, apparitions, mirages and hallucinations which those who attempt to perform such acts *by purely human means* cannot fail to encounter.

All true alchemists know alchemical symbols are chimeras just as theatre is a chimera. And this eternal reference to the fundamental principles and objects in theatre, found in almost all alchemist texts, ought to be understood as a feeling (the alchemists being extraordinarily conscious of it) of the similarity there is between the level on which characters, objects, portrayals and in a general way everything which makes up theatre's *virtual reality* develops, and the purely assumed, dreamlike level on which alchemist signs are evolved.

These symbols which indicate what might be called philosophical states of matter already set the mind on its way towards that fiery rarefaction, the unifying process of atrophy of nature's molecules in a horribly uncomplicated and filtrated sense. Towards that operation of the mind which, by dint of destructive analysis, rethinks and reconstitutes solids along these mentally balanced lines, whence they finally turn into gold. We do not understand sufficiently well how much the physical symbolism used to denote this secret work answers a like symbolism in the mind, putting ideas and appearances to work, by means of which everything theatrical in theatre is identified and is philosophically recognizable.

Let me explain. You may have already understood that the type of theatre we are referring to has nothing to do with the kind of social or topical theatre that changes with the times, where those ideas which originally put life into theatre are no longer found except in travestied gestures, unrecognizable, their meaning is so changed. Some ideas in typical, primal theatre have, like words, stopped having any effect and, instead of acting as diffusing agents, are now only a dead end and a mental tomb.

Perhaps, before I go any further, you might ask me to define what we mean by primal, archetypal theatre. Here we are getting to the heart of the matter.

If in fact we ask ourselves how theatre originated and why it was born (or why it was of prime importance), on the one hand we find a metaphysical substantiation or rather externalization of a kind of basic drama containing the fundamental bases of all drama in both a singular and diverse manner, themselves already *directed* and *divided*, not enough to lose their nature as first principles, but enough to have a panorama of endless clashes within them in an active, positive manner, that is, full of discharges, infinite perspectives of conflicts. One cannot analyse such drama philosophically, one can only do so purely poetically by seizing on whatever magnetic communications the fundamental principles all arts may contain that we can evoke in forms, sound, music and areas, through all the natural, pictorial replicas and likenesses, not in the mind's primordial courses, which our logical, excessive intellectualism would only reduce to useless outlines, but states whose keenness is so intense and so total that we feel the underlying threat of chaos through their quivering music and forms, as decisive as it is dangerous.

We feel this basic drama exists, made in the likeness of something subtler than Genesis itself and we ought to think of it as the result of one general – *unconflicting* – Will.

We must be led to think fundamental drama, a basis of all the Mysteries, is wedded to the second stage of Genesis, the time of obstacles and the Double, of matter and dulling of ideas.

It certainly seems wherever simplicity and order reign, there can be no drama or theatre, and that true theatre, just like poetry but by other means, is born from organized anarchy, after philosophical struggles which are the thrilling aspect of these aboriginal unifications.

Yet these clashes proposed by a Cosmos in turmoil in a philosophically corrupted, impure way are offered to us by alchemy in the strictest intellectuality, since they allow us to reach the sublime once more, only *dramatically*, after an enraged and scrupulous pounding of all insufficiently refined and matured forms. For it is in the nature of alchemy not to let the mind take flight until it has passed through all the channels and bedrock of existing matter, to redouble this labour in the future's white-hot limbo. We could say that in order to deserve tangible gold, the mind must first prove itself capable of the other it would have attained, would have reached, only by assenting to it, by considering it as a second symbol of the fall it had to undergo to rediscover the expression of light, rarity and intransmutability in a solid, impenetrable manner.

The dramatic act of making gold, because of the colossal conflicts it produces, because of the stupendous numbers of powers it arouses and hurls against one another, because of its call to a kind of basic redistillation overflowing with effects and overfull of spirituality, at last evoking absolute, abstract purity in the mind, where beyond it nothing more exists, which we might think of as a single note, a kind of defining note caught on the wing, like an organic part of indescribable vibration.

The Orphic Dithyrambs which captivated Plato must have had some of the transcendental, final aspects of *alchemist theatre* on an ethical, psychological level, coupled with factors of phenomenal psychological concentration, and conversely must have evoked alchemist signs, giving them the mental means of sifting and transfusing matter, evoking the mind's fiery, decisive transfusion.

We are told the Eleusinian Mysteries confined themselves to staging a certain number of eternal truths. I would say they must rather have staged projections and precipitations of indescribable struggles and clashes between first principles, taken from that giddy, slippery angle where all reality disappears by putting into effect the involved, unique fusion of the abstract and the empirical. I believe that we have lost any idea of their instrumental and musical notation, combining colours and forms by which on the one hand they must have gratified a nostalgia for pure beauty which Plato must have found at least once in this complete, resonant, streaming, naked realization, and on the other hand, resolved strange combinations inconceivable to our waking minds, to resolve or even to extirpate all conflicts produced by the antagonism between mind and matter, ideas and forms, abstract and concrete, to fuse all outward appearance in one single expression that must have resembled distilled gold.

On the Balinese Theatre*

The first Balinese theatre show derived from dance, singing, mime and music – but extraordinarily little from psychological theatre such as we understand it in Europe, re-establishing theatre as pure and independent creativity whose products are hallucination and terror.*

It is most remarkable that the first of the short plays in this spectacle shows us a father admonishing his custom-flouting daughter and begins with the entrance of ghosts. Or rather, the male and female characters who are going to enact the unfolding of this stock dramatic theme first appear as characters in ghostly form, and are seen in the guise of an illusion proper to all dramatic characters, before allowing any development in the situations of this kind of figurative sketch. Anyway, the situations only serve as a pretext in this case and the play does not develop through the emotions but through states of mind, themselves stilted and epitomized in gestures – outlines. In short, the Balinese produce the idea of pure theatre with the greatest exactness, where everything in concept and production is valued and only exists through the degree of its objectification *on stage*. They triumphantly demonstrate the absolute superiority of the producer whose creative ability *does away with words*. The themes are very general, indefinite and abstract. Only a complex expansion of stage artifice brings them to life, imposing on our minds something like the idea of a metaphysics coined from a new usage of gestures and speech.

In fact the strange thing about all these gestures, these angular, sudden, jerky postures, these syncopated inflections formed at the back of the throat, these musical phrases cut short, the sharded flights, rustling branches, hollow drum sounds, robot creaking, animated puppets dancing, is the feeling of a new bodily language no longer based on words but on signs which emerges through the maze of gestures, postures, airborne cries, through their gyrations and turns, leaving not even the smallest area of stage space unused. Those actors with their asymmetrical robes looking like moving hieroglyphs; not just the shape of their gowns, shifting the axis of the human figure, but creating a kind of second symbolic clothing standing beside the uniforms of those warriors entranced and perpetually at war, thus inspiring intellectual ideas or merely connecting all the criss-crossing of these lines with all the criss-crossing of spatial perspective. These mental signs have an exact meaning that only strikes one intuitively, but violently enough to make any translations into logical, discursive language useless. And for lovers of out-and-out realism, who might grow tired of the constant allusions to hidden, out-of-the-way attitudes of mind, there is still the double's nobly realistic acting, terrified as he is by apparitions from the Other World. There is a delineation of fear valid for all latitudes in this double who, by his trembling, childish yelping and heels striking the ground in time with the very automatism of the unleashed subconscious, hides behind his own reality, showing us that in human as well as in superhuman fields, Orientals are more than a match for us in matters of realism.

The Balinese, with gestures and a variety of mime to suit all occasions in life, reinstate the superior value of theatre conventions, demonstrate the effectiveness and greater active value of a certain number of well-learnt and above all masterfully applied conventions. One of the reasons for our delight in this faultless show lies precisely in the use these actors make of an exact amount of assured gesture, tried-and-tested mime coming in at an appointed place, but particularly in the mental clothing, in the deep, detailed study which governs the formulation of the expressive interplay of these effective signs, giving us the impression their effectiveness has not become weakened over the centuries. That mechanical eye-rolling, those pouting lips, the use of twitching muscles producing studiously calculated effects which prevent any resorting to spontaneous improvisation, those heads moving horizontally, seeming to slide from one shoulder to the other as if on rollers, all that corresponds to direct psychological needs as well as to a kind of mental construction made up of gestures, mime, the evocative power of rhythm, the musical quality of physical movement, the comparable, wonderfully fused harmony of a note. This may shock our European sense of stage freedom and spontaneous inspiration, but let no one say their precision makes for sterility or monotony. We get a marvellous feeling of richness, fantasy and bounteous lavishness emanating from this show regulated with a maddeningly conscious attention to detail. And the most impulsive correlations constantly fuse sight with sound, intellect with sensibility, a character's gestures with the evocation of a plant's movements through the aid of an instrumental cry. The sighs of a wind instrument prolong the vibrations of vocal cords so identically we do not know whether the voice itself is held, or the senses which first assimilated that voice. Those rippling joints, the musical angle the arm makes with a forearm, a falling foot, an arching knee, fingers that seem to come loose from the hand, all this is like a constant play of mirrors where human limbs seem to echo one another, harmonious orchestral notes and the whisper of wind instruments conjure up the idea of a passionate aviary where the actors themselves are the fluttering wings. Our theatre has never grasped this gestured metaphysics nor known how to make use of music for direct, concrete, dramatic purposes, our purely verbal theatre unaware of the sum total of theatre, of everything that exists spatially on the boards or is measured and circumscribed in space, having spatial density (moves, forms, colours, vibrations, postures, shouts), could learn a lesson in spirituality from the Balinese theatre with regard to the indeterminable, to dependence on the mind's suggestive power. This purely popular, non-religious theatre gives us an extraordinary idea of a nation's intellectual level, which takes the struggle of a soul as prey to the spectres and phantoms of the Other World to be the basis for its civic festivals. For the last part of the show certainly deals with purely inner conflicts. And in passing we ought to note the extent of theatrical magnificence the Balinese have been able to impart to it. The sense of the stage's plastic requirements are seen to be equalled only by their knowledge of physical fear and how to unleash it. And there is a striking similarity between the truly terrifying look of their devil, probably of Tibetan origin, and a certain puppet with leafy-green nails, its hands distended with white gelatine, the finest ornament of one of the first plays of the Alfred Jarry Theatre.*

* * *

This show is more than we can approach head on, bombarding us as it does with an overabundance of impressions each one more splendid than the last, but in a language to which we no longer seem to hold the key, and a kind of annoyance is caused by being unable to run it to earth or rediscover the thread, to turn one's ear closer to the instrument to hear it better, just one more charm to add to the show's credit. And by language I do not mean an idiom we fail to catch at first hearing, but precisely that kind of theatrical language foreign to every *spoken language*, where it seems a tremendous stage experience is recaptured, beside which our exclusively dialogue productions seem like so much stammering.

In fact, the most striking thing about this show – so well-contrived to baffle our Western concept of theatre that many may well deny it any dramatic qualities, whereas it is the finest demonstration of pure theatre we have ever been privileged to see here – what is striking and disturbing about it for us as Europeans is the wonderful intelligence seeming to spark through the compact texture of gestures, in the infinitely varied voice inflections, in that tempest of sound resounding as if from a vast, dripping rainforest, and in the equally sonorous interlacing moves. There is no transition from a gesture to a cry or a sound; everything is connected as if through strange channels penetrating right through the mind!

There is a horde of ritual gestures in it to which we have no key, seeming to obey a very precise, musical indication, with something added that does not usually belong to music and seems to be aimed at encircling thought, hounding it down, leading it into a sure, labyrinthine system. In fact everything in this theatre is assessed with loving, unerring attention to detail. Nothing is left either to chance or individual initiative. It is a kind of sublime dance where the dancers are actors first and foremost.

We see them repeatedly carry out a kind of reanimation at a measured tread. Just as they appear to be lost in a hopelessly intricate maze of beats and we feel they are about to fall prey to confusion, they have their own way of regaining their balance, a peculiar arching, leg-twisting stance which gives the impression of a wet cloth about to be wrung to music – suddenly the floating rhythm ends, the beat becomes clear on three final steps, inevitably bringing them back to centre stage.

Everything is just as ordered and just as impersonal with them. Not one rippling muscle, not one rolling eye does not seem to belong to a kind of deliberate accuracy directing everything, through which everything happens. The odd thing is that in this systematic depersonalization, in the purely muscular facial expressions, like feature masks, everything produces, conveys the utmost effect.

41

We are seized with a kind of terror when we think of these mechanical beings whose happiness and pain seem not to be their own, but to obey tried-and-tested rituals as if governed by higher intellects. In the last analysis, this impression of a higher, controlled life is what strikes us most about this show, like a profane ritual. It has the solemnity of a holy ritual – the hieratic costumes give each actor a kind of dual body, dual limbs – and in his costume, the stiff stilted artist seems merely his own effigy. Beside the booming, pounding musical rhythm – there is a sustained hesitating fragile music which seems to grind the most precious metals, where springs of water bubble up as in a state of nature, where columns of insects march through the plants, where the sound of light itself appears to have been picked up, where the sounds of deep solitudes seem distilled into crystal swarms.

Furthermore, all these sounds are linked to movements, they are like the natural conclusion of gestures with the same attributes. All this with such a feeling of musical similarity, the mind is at last obliged to confuse them, attributing the sound qualities of the orchestra to the artist's articulated gesticulation – and vice versa.

An inhuman, sacred, miraculously revealing impression emanates from the exquisite beauty of the women's headdress, a series of radiant tiers made up of arrangements of multicoloured feathers, from pearls so lovely their colouring, their variegation seems so justly to have been *revealed*, the crests tremble rhythmically, seeming *consciously* to answer the trembling bodies. There are also the other headdresses of a priestly appearance, in tiara form, topped with egret crests and tufts of stiff flowers in pairs of contrasting, strangely harmonized colours.

This throbbing ensemble, full of rockets, flights, canals, detours in all the directions of our inner and outer perception, creates theatre as a sovereign idea such as it has been preserved for us through the ages, to teach us what it ought never to have stopped being. And this impression is increased by the fact that this show – popular out there, it seems, and profane – is like the daily bread of these people's artistic feelings.*

Aside from this show's stupendous precision, the thing which seems to surprise and astonish us the most is this *revealing aspect of matter*, suddenly seeming to disperse in signs, to teach us the metaphysical identity of abstract and concrete and to teach it to us in *lasting* *gestures.* For though we are familiar with its realistic aspect, here it is raised to the *n*th power and absolutely stylized.*

All creativity stems from the stage in this drama, finding its expression and even its sources in a secret psychic impulse, speech prior to words.*

This theatre does away with the playwright to the advantage of what in Western theatre jargon we call the producer. But the latter becomes a kind of organizer of magic, a master of holy ceremonies. And the material on which he works, the subjects he makes thrilling are not his own, but descend from the gods. They seem to stem from primal unions in Nature promoted by a double Spirit.*

What he sets in motion is MANIFEST.

A kind of ancient Natural Philosophy, from which the mind has never been separated.

There is something about a spectacle like Balinese theatre which does away with entertainment, that aspect of useless artificiality, an evening's amusement so typical of our own theatre. Its productions are hewn out of matter itself before our eyes, in real life itself. There is something of a religious ritual ceremony about them, in the sense that they eradicate any idea of pretence, a ridiculous imitation of real life, from the spectator's mind. This involved gesticulation we see has a goal, an immediate goal towards which it aims by effective means, and we are able to experience its direct effectiveness. The thought it aims at, the states of mind it attempts to create, the mystical discoveries it offers are motivated and reached without delay or periphrasis. It all seems like an exorcism to make our devils FLOW.

This theatre vibrates with instinctive things,* but brought to that lucid, intelligent, malleable point where they seem physically to supply us with some of the mind's most secret perceptions.*

We might say the subjects presented begin on stage. They have reached such a point of objective materialization we could not imagine them, however much one might try, outside this compact panorama, the enclosed, confined world of the stage.

This show gives us a wonderful compound of pure stage imagery and a whole new language seems to have been invented in order to

43

make it understood. The actors and costumes form true, living, moving hieroglyphs. And these three-dimensional hieroglyphics are in turn embellished with a certain number of gestures, strange signs matching some dark prodigious reality we have repressed once and for all here in the West.

There is something of the state of mind of a magic act in this intensive liberation of signs, at first held back, then abruptly launched into the air.

Confused seething, full of recognizable particles at times strangely orderly, sparkles in the effervescence of these painted rhythms, where the fermatas constantly play and are interposed like calculated silences.

But no one in the West has ever tried to bring this concept of pure theatre to life, since we regard it as merely theoretical, whereas the Balinese theatre offers us an outstanding production that suppresses any likelihood of recourse to words to clarify the most abstract subjects; it has invented a language of gestures to be spatially developed, but having no meaning outside it.

The stage is used in all its dimensions, one might even say on all possible levels. For besides a keen sense of plastic beauty, these gestures are always ultimately aimed at the clarification of a state of mind or mental problem.

At least that is how it appears to us.

No point in space, and at the same time no possible intimations are wasted. And there is something like a philosophical feeling of the power nature has to rush suddenly headlong into chaos.

In Balinese theatre one senses a state prior to language, able to select its own language: music, gestures, moves and words.

We can be sure this aspect of pure theatre, this natural philosophy of total gesture, an idea in itself, transforming the mind's persuasions in order to be discerned through the fibrous maze and tangle of matter, gives us a new idea of whatever properly belongs to the field of form and visible matter. Anyone who succeeds in imparting a mystical meaning to the simple outline of a gown, not simply content with placing man beside his Double, but ascribing to each costumed person their costumed double – those who run these phantasmal clothes, these second clothes,

44

through with a sword, giving them the look of huge butterflies pinned in the air, these people have a far more inborn sense than us of nature's total, occult symbolism, teaching us a lesson which we can be only too sure our theatre technicians would be incapable of using.

The intellectual space, psychic interplay and silence solidified by thought existing between the parts of a written sentence are drawn on stage between the parts, areas and sight lines of a certain number of shouts, colours and moves.

In the Balinese theatre productions the mind certainly gets the feeling that concepts clashed with gestures first, establishing themselves among a whole ferment of sight and sound imagery, thoughts as it were in a pure state. To sum it up more distinctly, something like a musical condition must have existed to produce this staging, where everything that is imagined by the mind is only an excuse, a virtuality whose double produced this intense scenic poetry, this many-hued spatial language.

This constantly mirrored interplay, passing from a colour to a gesture, from cries to movements, endlessly leads us along rough paths that are difficult for the mind, pitching us into that uncertainty, that indescribably anxious state most suited to poetry.

A kind of awful fixation emanates from the strange rippling of flying hands, like insects in the green night, an inexhaustible mental rationalization, as if the mind were perpetually busy getting its bearings within the maze of its own subconscious.

Besides, the things this theatre makes tangible are much less emotional than intellectual, enclosing them as it does within concrete, though almost constantly esoteric signs.

Thus we are led along intellectual paths towards reconquering the signs of existence.

From this point of view the star dancer's gesture is highly significant, always touching the same spot on his head as he does, as if he wanted to mark the place and existence of some focal mind's eye.

Something which is a highly coloured allusion to physical impressions of nature recaptures them on a sensory level, the sound itself being only a nostalgic image of something else, a kind of magic state where feelings have become so sensitive they are suitable for visitation by the mind. Even the imitative harmonies, the sound of a rattlesnake for instance or insect shells splintering against one another, evoke the clearing in a teeming landscape ready to hurl itself into chaos. And those performers dressed in dazzling costumes whose bodies underneath them seemed wrapped in swaddling clothes! There is something umbilical, larval about their movements. At the same time we ought to note the hieroglyphic appearance of the costumes, the horizontal lines extending out beyond the body in all directions. They are like giant insects covered with lines and segments made to unite them with unknown natural perspectives of which they appear as nothing more than its untangented geometry.

These costumes which encircle their abstract sliding walk, the strange criss-crossing of their feet!

Every one of their moves draws a line in space, an unknown meticulous figure of predetermined hermeticism, which an unforeseen gesture completes.

And the folds of these robes curving above their buttocks, holding them up as if suspended in the air, as if pinned onto the backdrop, prolonging each of their leaps into flight.

Those howls, those rolling eyes, that unceasing abstraction, those sounds of branches, of chopping and log-rolling, all in a vast expanse of sounds flowing out from several outlets at once, all combine to give rise in our minds, to crystallize a new concept, what one might term a concrete concept of the abstract.

It is worth noting that this abstraction, which originates in a wonderful stage construction, to return into thought, when it encounters impressions of the natural world in motion, it always grasps them at the point where they penetrate their molecular grouping. That is to say, only a gesture narrowly keeps us from chaos.

The last part of the show is divinely anachronistic when compared with everything that is dirty, brutish and ignominiously chewed up on the European stage. And I do not know any theatre that would *naturalistically* dare to pin down the horrors of a soul as prey to the ghosts of the Other World in this way.*

These metaphysicians of natural chaos dance, restoring every iota of sound, each fragmentary perception, as if it were ready to return to its origins, able to wed movement and sound so perfectly it seems the dancers have hollow limbs to make sounds of wood blocks, resounding drums and echoing instruments with their hollow, wooden limbs.

Here we are suddenly in the thick of a metaphysical struggle and the rigid aspect of the body in a trance, tensed by the surging of the cosmic powers attacking it, is admirably expressed in that frenzied dance full of angular stiffness, where we suddenly feel the mind's headlong fall begins.

They seem like substantial waves, dashing their crests into the deep, and rushing from all points of the horizon to hurtle themselves into an infinitesimal portion of a quivering trance – to cover the void of fear.

There is something absolute about these spatial constructions, the kind of true physical absolute only Orientals can envisage – for they differ from our European theatre concepts in the sublimity and the considered daring of their aims even more than in the strange perfection of their productions.

Supporters of classifications and dividing into categories may pretend to see mere dancers in Balinese theatre's magnificent performers, dancers entrusted with portraying some great Myth or other whose sublimity makes the level of modern Western theatre unspeakably crude and childish. The truth is that Balinese theatre offers and brings us already produced pure dramatic subjects, while the stage setting bestows a concentrated balance on it, a wholly substantiated attraction.*

All of this is steeped in deep intoxication, restoring the very elements of rapture, and in this rapture we rediscover the dry seething and mineral friction of plants, remains and ruined trees frontally illuminated.

All bestiality and animalism are brought down to that dry gesture, striking sounds as the earth splits open, frozen trees, lowing animals.

The dancers' feet, by that gesture of parting their robes, dissolve thoughts and feelings, returning them to their pure state.

And always confronting the head, that Cyclops eye, the inner mind's eye sought by that right hand.

Miming, mental gestures, accenting, curtailing, settling, dividing and subdividing feelings, soul states and metaphysical ideas.

This quintessent theatre where objects about-face strangely before returning to abstraction.

Their gestures fall so exactly on that woody, hollow drum rhythm, accenting it, grasping it in flight so assuredly, on such summits, it seems this music accents the very void in their hollow limbs.

The women's stratified, lunar eyes.

Those dreamlike eyes appearing to engulf us, before which we see ourselves as *ghosts*.

Utterly satisfying dance gestures, turning feet mingling with soul states, those tiny flying hands, the dry, precise tapping.

We watch mental alchemy creating a gesture out of a state of mind, the dry, naked, linear gestures our acts might have if they sought the absolute.

It happens that these mannerisms, this profuse hieratism with its sliding alphabet, its shrieks of creaking stones, branch sounds, where chopping and log-rolling fashion a kind of moving audio-visual substantiated murmuring in the air, in space. And after a moment the magical identification has occurred: WE KNOW WE ARE SPEAKING.

Who, after Arjuna's titanic battle with the Dragon, dares say all theatre is not on stage, that is to say, beyond situations and words.

For here, the psychological and dramatic situations have gone into the very mime of the fight, a function of the mystical, athletic acting of their bodies, I might even say the undulatory use of the stage, whose gigantic spiral is disclosed step by step.

The warriors enter the mental forest slithering in fear. A great shudder, something like a prodigious magnetic vertigo overcomes them, and we feel inhuman or mineral meteorites hurtling down on them.

The general trembling in their limbs and their rolling eyes signify more than a physical storm or mental concussion. The sensory pulsing of their bristling heads is excruciating at times – and that music behind them which sways and nourishes some unknown space or other where actual stones finally stop rolling.

And behind the Warrior, beset by the fearful cosmic storm, stands the Double giving himself airs, given up to the childishness of his schoolboy gibes, who, aroused by the repercussions of the surging gale, moves unaware in the midst of uncomprehended charms.

Oriental and Western Theatre*

Balinese theatre was not a revelation of a verbal but a physical idea of theatre where drama is encompassed within the limits of everything that can happen on stage, independently of a written script. Whereas with us, the lines gain the upper hand and theatre as we understand it finds itself restricted by them. Thus theatre is a branch of literature, a species of vocal language, and even if we admit a difference between the lines spoken on stage and those read by the eyes, even if we confine theatre to what goes on between the cues, we will never succeed in divorcing theatre from the idea of script production.

This notion, the predominance of the lines in theatre, is deeply rooted in us and we view theatre so much as just a physical reflection of the script, that everything in theatre outside the script, not contained within its limits or strictly determined by it, appears to us to be a part of staging, and inferior to the script.

Given the subservience of theatre to the lines, we might ask ourselves whether theatre by any chance possesses a language of its own, or whether it would really be illusory to consider it an independent, autonomous art for the same reasons as music, painting, dance, etc.

In any case if such a language exists it will inevitably be confused with staging viewed:

1. On the one hand as the lines visually, plastically materialized.

2. On the other, as a language expressing everything which can be said or intended on stage distinct from the lines, everything that can be spatially embodied, affected or disrupted by it.

Once we consider this production language as theatre's pure language, we must discover whether it is capable of attaining the same inner object as the words, whether from a theatrical or mental viewpoint it can claim the same intellectual effectiveness as spoken language. In other words we must not ask ourselves whether it can define thought but whether it *makes us think*, and leads the mind to assume deeply effective attitudes from its own point of view.

In short, if one questions the intellectual effectiveness of expression through objective forms, of a language using forms, sound and gesture, one is questioning the intellectual effectiveness of art.

Although we have come to credit art with nothing more than a pleasurable relaxing value, confining it to the purely express use of forms, to the compatibility between certain surface relationships, this in no way diminishes its deeply expressive value. But the mental weakness of the West, where man has especially confused art and aesthetics, is to believe one can have painting used only as painting, dancing as a plastic form alone, as if one wanted to cut art off from everything, to sever the links with all the mystical attitudes they might adopt in confrontation with the absolute.

One therefore understands that theatre, inasmuch as it remains confined within its own language and in correlation with it, must make a break with topicality. It is not aimed at solving social or psychological conflicts, to serve as a battlefield for moral passions, but to express objectively secret truths, to bring out in active gestures those elements of truth hidden under forms in their encounters with Becoming.

To do that, to link theatre with expressive form potential, with everything in the way of gestures, sound, colours, movement, is to return it to its original purpose, to restore it to a religious, metaphysical position, to reconcile it with the universe.

But while one might say words have their own metaphysical power, no one says we cannot think of speech as well as gestures on a universal level. Besides, it is more effective on this level as a dissociating force exerted on material appearances, as on all states in which the mind feels settled or tends to relax. We can readily answer that this metaphysical way of looking at dialogue is not used in Western theatre since it does not make it an active power springing from the destruction of appearances to reach the mind, but on the contrary uses it as a final degree of thought, lost in being externalized.

In Western theatre, words are solely used to express psychological conflicts peculiar to man and his position in everyday existence. His conflicts are clearly justifiable in spoken words, and whether they remain in the psychological field, or leave it to pass over into the social field, drama will always concern morality owing to the way in which conflicts attack and disrupt character. And this will always remain in a field where words, verbal solutions, retain their advantage. But these moral conflicts, by their very nature, do not need to be resolved on stage. To make speech or verbal expression dominant over the objective expressiveness of gestures and everything on stage spatially affecting the mind through the senses means turning our backs on the physical requirements of the stage and rebelling against its potential.

We must admit theatre's sphere is physical and plastic, not psychological. This does not simply mean assessing whether theatre's physical language can attain the same psychological resolutions as words or whether it can express emotions and feelings as well as words, but whether there are not attitudes in the field of intellect and thought which words cannot assume, which gestures and everything inclusive in this spatial language cannot attain with greater precision than them.

Before giving any examples of connections between the physical world and profound states of mind, I will quote what I wrote elsewhere:

> Any true feeling cannot in reality be expressed. To do so is to betray it. To express it, however, is to *conceal* it. True expression conceals what it exhibits. It pits the mind against nature's real vacuum, by creating in reaction a kind of fullness of thought. Or rather it creates a vacuum in thought, in relation to the manifest illusion of nature. Any strong feeling produces an idea of emptiness within us, and lucid language which prevents this emptiness also prevents poetry appearing in thought. For this reason an image, an allegory, a form disguising what it means to reveal, has more meaning to the mind than the enlightenment brought about by words or their analysis.
>
> Hence true beauty never strikes us directly and the setting sun is beautiful because of everything else we lose by it.*

The nightmares in Flemish painting are striking because they juxtapose the real world with a mere caricature of the world. They present us with spectres we encounter in our dreams. They originate in those same dream states which cause clumsy gestures and ridiculous slips of the tongue. They place a leaping harp beside a forgotten child; they show a real army advancing beneath the walls of a redoubtable fortress beside a human embryo carried along by underground rapids. Beside dreamt perplexity is the march of certainty, beyond yellow cavernous light the orange flash of a huge autumn sun about to set.

There is no question of abolishing speech in theatre but of changing its intended purpose, especially to lessen its status, to view it as something other than a way of guiding human nature to external ends, since our theatre is solely concerned with the way emotions and feelings conflict with one another or the way man is set against man in life.

Yet to change the purpose of theatre dialogue is to use it in an actual spatial sense, uniting it with everything in theatre that is spatial and significant in the tangible field. This means handling it as something concrete, disturbing things, first spatially, then in an infinitely more secret and mysterious field permitting more scope. And it is not very hard to identify this extensive yet secretive field with that of formal anarchy on the one hand and also constant, formal creation on the other.

Thus, this identification of theatre's object with every possibility of formal, extensive manifestation gives rise to the idea of a kind of spatial poetry, itself confused with enchantment.

In Oriental theatre with its metaphysical tendencies, as compared with Western theatre with its psychological tendencies, forms assume their meaning and significance on all possible levels. Or if you like, their pulsating results are not inferred merely on one level but on all mental levels at once.

And because of their manifold aspects, their disruptive strength and charm constantly stimulate the mind. Because Oriental theatre accepts the external appearance of things on several levels, because it does not restrict itself solely to the limitations or the impact of these aspects on the senses, but instead examines the degree of mental potential from which they have emerged, it shares in the intense poetry of nature and preserves its magical relationship with all the objective stages of universal mesmerism.

We ought to consider staging from the angle of magic and enchantment, not as reflecting a script, the mere projection of actual doubles arising from writing, but as the fiery projection of all the objective results of gestures, words, sounds, music or their combinations. This active projection can only occur on stage and its results can only be discovered from the auditorium or stage. And a playwright who uses nothing but words is not needed and must give way to specialists in objective, animated enchantment.

No More Masterpieces*

One of the reasons for the stifling atmosphere we live in, without any possible escape or remedy, which is shared by even the most revolutionary among us – is our respect for what has been written, expressed or painted, for whatever has taken shape, as if all expression were not finally exhausted, has not arrived at the point where things must break up to begin again, to make a fresh start.

We must finally do away with the idea of masterpieces reserved for a so-called elite but incomprehensible to the masses, since the mind has no red-light districts like those used for illicit sexual relations.

Past masterpieces are fit for the past, they are no good to us. We have the right to say what has been said and even what has not been said in a way that belongs to us, responding in a direct and straightforward manner to present-day feelings everybody can understand.

It is senseless to criticize the masses for having no sense of the sublime, when we ourselves confuse the sublime with one of those formal, moreover always dead, exhibits. And if, for example, the masses today no longer understand *Oedipus Rex*, I would venture to say *Oedipus Rex* is at fault as a play and not the masses.

In *Oedipus Rex* there is the incest theme and the idea that nature does not give a rap for morality. And there are wayward powers at large we would do well to be aware of, call them *fate* or what you will.

In addition, there is the presence of a plague epidemic which is the physical incarnation of these powers. But all this is clothed in language which has lost any contact with today's crude, epileptic rhythm. Sophocles may speak nobly, but in a manner that no longer suits the times. His speeches are too refined for today, as if he were speaking beside the point.

Yet the masses tremble at railway disasters, are familiar with earthquakes, plagues, revolutions and wars as well as being sensitive to the disturbing anguish of love and are capable of becoming conscious of all those grand ideas. They ask only to become conscious of them, but on condition we know how to speak their language and that notions of these things are not brought to them invested in a sophistication belonging to dead periods we will never relive.

Just as in former times, the masses today are thirsting for mystery. They only ask to become conscious of the laws by which fate reveals itself and perhaps to guess at the secret of its apparitions.

Let us leave textual criticism to teachers and formal criticism to aesthetes, and acknowledge that what has already been said no longer needs saying; that an expression twice used is of no value since it does not have two lives. Once spoken, all speech is dead and is only active as it is spoken. Once a form is used it has no more use, bidding man find another form, and theatre is the only place in the world where a gesture, once made, is never repeated in the same way.

If the masses do not frequent literary masterpieces, this is because the masterpieces are literary, that is to say set in forms no longer answering the needs of the times.

Far from accusing the masses, the public, we must accuse the formal screen we place between ourselves and the masses and that form of a new idolatry, the idolizing of set masterpieces, an aspect of middle-class conformity.

The conformity that makes us confuse the sublime, the concepts, and the objects with the forms they have acquired in our minds through the ages – our affected, snobbish, aesthetic mentality, which the public no longer understands.

It is useless in all this to accuse the public's bad taste while it slakes its thirst with inanities, as long as we have not given the public a worth-while show. And I defy anyone to point out a worthwhile show *here*, worthwhile in the highest sense of theatre, since the last great Romantic melodramas, that is, a hundred years ago.

The public, which mistakes the bogus for truth, has the sense of what is true and always reacts to it when it appears. Today, however, we must look for it in the street, not on stage. And if the crowds in the street were given a chance to show their dignity as human beings, they would always do so.

If the masses have grown unused to going to the theatre, if we have all finally come to regard theatre as an inferior art, a means of coarse distraction, using it as an outlet for our worst instincts, this is because we have for too long been told theatre is all lies and illusion. Because for four hundred years, that is, since the Renaissance, we have become accustomed to purely descriptive, narrative theatre, narrating psychology.

People exerted their ingenuity to bring to life on stage credible but detached beings, with the show on one side and the masses on the other – and the masses were shown only a mirror of themselves.

Shakespeare himself is responsible for this aberration and decline, this isolationist concept of theatre, holding that a stage performance ought not to affect the public, or that a projected image should not cause a shock to the anatomy, leaving an indelible impression on it.

If man in Shakespeare's plays is sometimes concerned with what is above him, it is always finally to determine the result of that concern within man, that is, psychology.

Psychology persists in bringing the unknown down to a level with the known, that is to say with the everyday and pedestrian. And psychology has caused this abasement and fearful loss of energy which appears to me to have really reached its limit. And it seems both theatre and ourselves want nothing more to do with psychology.

Besides, I think we are all agreed on this point of view, and in order to censure psychological drama there is no need to stoop as low as disgusting modern French theatre.

Plots dealing with money, money troubles, social climbing, the pangs of love unspoilt by altruism, sexuality sugar-coated with eroticism yet shorn of mystery, are not theatre even if they are psychology. This anxiety, debauchery and lust, before which we are only Peeping Toms gratifying our instincts, tends to go sour and turn into revolution. This is something we must realize.

But that is not our most serious concern.

In the long run, Shakespeare and his followers have instilled a concept of art for art's sake in us, art on the one hand and life on the other, and we might rely on this lazy, ineffective idea as long as life outside held good, but there are too many signs that everything which used to sustain our lives no longer does so and we are all mad, desperate and sick. And I urge *us* to react.

This concept of unworldly art, charm poetry existing solely to charm away the hours, is a decadent notion, an unmistakable symptom of the emasculatory force within us.

Our literary admiration for Rimbaud, Jarry, Lautréamont and a few others, which drove two men to suicide, but turned into nothing more than café chit-chat for the rest, belongs to the idea of literary poetry, detached art, emasculated mental activity which has no effect and produces nothing. And I note that just when personal poetry, involving only its creator as he creates, became rife in a most excessive way, theatre was held in great contempt by poets who never had either a feeling for immediate group action, effectiveness or danger.

Let us do away with this foolish adherence to texts, to *written* poetry. Written poetry is valid once and then ought to be torn up. Let dead poets make way for the living. And we ought after all to be able to see it is our adulation for what has already been done, however fine and worthy it may be, that fossilizes us, makes us stagnate and prevents us contacting that underlying power called thinking energy, vital power, determination of exchange, lunar periods or what have you. Poetry plain and simple, unformed and unwritten, underlies textual poetry. And just as masks, once used in magic rituals, are no longer fit for anything but to be put in museums – in the same way, the poetic effectiveness of a text is exhausted – theatre's effectiveness and poetry is exhausted least quickly of all, since it permits the action of movement and spoken things, never reproduced twice.

We must know what we want. If we are all prepared for war, the plague, famine and slaughter, we have no need to say so, we have only to go on as we are. To go on behaving as snobs, to flock to hear such and such a singer, to see such and such a wonderful show which never transcends the world of art (even the *Ballets Russes* at the height of their splendour never transcended the world of art), such and such an exhibition of painting where impressive forms dazzle us here and there, only by chance, and without being truly conscious of the powers they could arouse.

This empiricism, chance, personalism and anarchy must come to an end.

No more personal poems benefiting those who write them more than those who read them.

Once and for all, enough of these displays of closed, conceited, personal art.

Our anarchy and mental confusion are a function of the anarchy of everything else – or rather everything else is a function of that anarchy.

I am not of the opinion that civilization must change so theatre can change, but I do believe theatre used in the highest and most difficult sense has the power to affect the appearance and structure of things. And bringing two impassioned revelations together on stage, two living fires, two nervous magnetisms, is just as complete, as true, even as decisive as bringing together two bodies in short-lived debauchery is in life.

For this reason I suggest a Theatre of Cruelty.

With this mania we all have today for belittling everything, as soon as I said "cruelty" everyone took it to mean "blood". But a "*theatre of cruelty*" means theatre that is difficult and cruel for myself first of all. And on the level of performance, it has nothing to do with the cruelty we practise on one another, hacking at each other's bodies, carving up our individual anatomies, or like ancient Assyrian Emperors, posting sackfuls of human ears, noses or neatly dissected nostrils, but the far more terrible, essential cruelty objects can practise on us. We are not free and the sky can still fall on our heads. And above all else, theatre is made to teach us this.

Either we will be able to revert through theatre by present-day means to the higher idea of poetry underlying the Myths told by the great tragedians of ancient times, with theatre able once more to sustain a religious concept, that is to say without any meditation or useless contemplation, without diffuse dreams, to become conscious and also be in command of certain predominant powers, certain ideas governing everything: and since ideas, when they are effective, generate their own energy, rediscover within us that energy which in the last analysis creates order and increases the value of life, or else we might as well abdicate now without protest, and acknowledge we are fit only for chaos, famine, bloodshed, war and epidemics.

Either we restore one focal attitude and necessity in all the arts, finding correspondences between a gesture in painting or on stage, and a gesture made by lava in a volcanic eruption, or we must stop painting, gossiping, writing or doing anything at all.

I suggest theatre today ought to return to the fundamental magic notion reintroduced by psychoanalysis, which consists in curing a patient by making him assume the external attitude of the desired condition.

I suggest we ought to reject the empiricism of random images produced by the subconscious, calling them poetic and therefore hermetic images, as if that kind of trance brought about by poetry does not reverberate throughout our whole sensibility, in every nerve, as if poetry were a shadowy power with invariable motions.

I suggest we ought to return through theatre to the idea of a physical knowledge of images, a means of inducing trances, just as Chinese medicine knows the points of acupuncture over the whole extent of the human anatomy, down to our most sensitive functions.

Theatre can reinstruct those who have forgotten the communicative power or magic mimicry of gesture, because a gesture contains its own energy, and there are still human beings in theatre to reveal the power of these gestures.

To practise art is to deprive a gesture of its reverberations throughout the anatomy, whereas these reverberations, if the gesture is made in the conditions and with the force required, impels the anatomy and, through it, the whole personality to adopt attitudes that correspond to that gesture.

Theatre is the only place in the world, the last group means we still possess of directly affecting the anatomy, and in neurotic, basely sensual periods like the one in which we are immersed, of attacking that base sensuality through physical means it cannot withstand.

Snakes do not react to music because of the mental ideas it produces in them, but because they are long, they lie coiled on the ground and their bodies are in contact with the ground along almost their entire length. And the musical vibrations communicated to the ground affect them as a very subtle, very long massage. Well, I propose to treat the audience just like those charmed snakes and to bring them back to the subtlest ideas through their anatomies.

First of all by crude means, these gradually becoming more refined. But these crude, direct means hold its attention from the start.

For this reason the audience is in the centre in the "Theatre of Cruelty", while the show takes place around them.

In such a show there is continual amplification; the sounds, noises and cries are first sought for their vibratory qualities, secondly for what they represent.

Lighting occurs in its turn in these progressively refined means. Lighting made not only to give colour or to shed light, but containing its own force, influence and suggestiveness. For light in a green cave does not predispose the organism sensually in the same way as light on a very windy day.

Following on from sound and lighting there is action and action's dynamism. This is where theatre, far from imitating life, communicates wherever it can with pure forces. And whether we accept or deny them, there is nonetheless a manner of speaking which gives the name "forces" to whatever gives birth to forceful images in our subconscious, to outwardly motiveless crime.

Violent, concentrated action is like lyricism; it calls forth supernatural imagery, a bloodshed of images, a bloody spurt of images inside the poet's head as well as in the audience's.

Whatever conflicts may obsess the mentality of the times, I defy any spectator infused with the blood of violent scenes, who has felt higher action pass through him, who has seen the rare, fundamental motions of his thought illuminated in extraordinary events – violence and bloodshed having been placed at the service of violence in thought – once outside the theatre, I defy him to indulge in thoughts of war, riot or motiveless murder.

The idea may seem puerile and advanced when stated in this way. And some will claim one example encourages another, that an attitude to cure encourages a cure, or murder to murder. Everything depends on the manner and purity with which things are done. There are risks. But we must not forget that while theatre action is violent, it is not biased, and theatre teaches us just how useless action is, since once it is done it is over, as well as the superior use of that state of mind unused by action but which, if *turned about*, sublimates.

Therefore I propose a theatre where violent physical images pulverize, mesmerize the audience's sensibilities, caught in the drama as if in a vortex of higher forces.

Theatre, abandoning psychology, must narrate the unusual, stage nature's conflicts, nature's subtle powers arising first and foremost as extraordinary derivative powers. Theatre bringing on trances just as the whirling Dervishes or the Assouas induce trances. It must be aimed at the system by exact means, the same means as the sympathetic music used by some tribes which we admire on records but are incapable of originating among ourselves.

One runs risks, but I consider that in present-day conditions they are worth running. I do not believe we have succeeded in reanimating the world we live in and I also do not believe it worth hanging on to. But I propose something to get us out of the slump, instead of continuing to moan about it, about the boredom, dullness and stupidity of everything.

Theatre and Cruelty*

We have lost the idea of theatre. And inasmuch as theatre restricts itself to probing the intimacy of a few puppets, thereby transforming the audience into Peeping Toms, one understands why the elite have turned away from it or why the masses go to the cinema, music hall and circus to find violent gratification whose intention does not disappoint them.

Our sensibility has reached the point where we surely need theatre that wakes us up, heart and nerves.

The damage wrought by psychological theatre, derived from Racine, has rendered us unaccustomed to the direct, violent action theatre must have. Cinema, in its turn, murders us with reflected, filtered and projected images that no longer *connect* with our sensibility, and for ten years has maintained us and all our faculties in an intellectual stupor.

In the anguished, catastrophic times we live in, we feel an urgent need for theatre that is not overshadowed by events, but arouses deep echoes within us and predominates over our unsettled period.

Our long-standing habit of seeking diversions has made us forget the slightest idea of serious theatre which upsets all our preconceptions, inspiring us with fiery, magnetic imagery and finally reacting on us after the manner of unforgettable soul therapy.

Everything that acts is cruelty. Theatre must rebuild itself on a concept of this drastic action pushed to the limit.

Infused with the idea that the masses think with their senses first and foremost and that it is ridiculous to appeal primarily to our understanding as we do in everyday psychological theatre, the Theatre of Cruelty proposes to resort to mass theatre, thereby rediscovering a little of the poetry in the ferment of great, agitated crowds hurled against one another, sensations only too rare nowadays, when masses of holiday crowds throng the streets.

If theatre wants to find itself needed once more, it must present everything in love, crime, war and madness.

Everyday love, personal ambition and daily worries are worthless except in relation to the kind of awful lyricism that exists in those Myths to which the great mass of men have consented.

This is why we will try to centre our show around famous personalities, horrible crimes and superhuman self-sacrifices, demonstrating that it can draw out the powers struggling within them, without resorting to the dead imagery of ancient Myths.

In a word, we believe there are living powers in what is called poetry, and that the picture of a crime presented in the right stage conditions is something infinitely more dangerous to the mind than if the same crime were committed in life.

We want to make theatre a believable reality inflicting this kind of tangible laceration, contained in all true feeling, on the heart and senses. In the same way as our dreams react on us and reality reacts on our dreams, so we believe ourselves able to associate mental pictures with dreams, effective insofar as they are projected with the required violence. And the audience will believe in the illusion of theatre on condition they really take it for a dream, not for a servile imitation of reality. On condition it releases the magic freedom of daydreams, only recognizable when imprinted with terror and cruelty.

Hence this full-scale invocation of cruelty and terror, its scope testing our entire vitality, confronting us with all our potential.

And in order to affect every facet of the spectator's sensibility, we advocate a revolving show, which, instead of making stage and auditorium into two closed worlds without any possible communication between them, will extend its visual and oral outbursts over the whole mass of spectators.

Furthermore, leaving the field of analysable emotional feelings aside, we intend using the actor's lyricism to reveal external powers, and by this means to bring the whole of nature into the kind of theatre we would like to evoke.

However extensive a programme of this kind may be, it does not overreach theatre itself, which all in all seems to us to be associated with ancient magic powers.

Practically speaking, we want to bring back the idea of total theatre, where theatre will recapture from cinema, music hall, the circus and life itself those things that always belonged to it. This division between analytical theatre and a world of movement seems stupid to us. One cannot separate body and mind, nor the senses from the intellect, particularly in a field where the unendingly repeated jading of our organs calls for sudden shocks to revive our understanding.

Thus on the one hand we have the magnitude and scale of a show aimed at the whole anatomy, and on the other an intensive mustering of objects, gestures and signs used in a new spirit. The reduced role given to understanding leads to drastic curtailment of the script, while the active role given to dark poetic feeling necessitates tangible signs. Words mean little to the mind; expanded areas and objects speak out. New imagery speaks, even if composed in words. But spatial, thundering images replete with sound also speak, if we become versed in arranging a sufficient interjection of spatial areas furnished with silence and stillness.

We expect to stage a show based on these principles, where these direct active means are wholly used. Therefore such a show, unafraid of exploring the limits of our nervous sensibility, uses rhythm, sound, words, resounding with song, whose nature and startling combinations are part of an unrevealed technique.

Moreover, to speak clearly, the imagery in some paintings by Grünewald or Hieronymus Bosch gives us a good enough idea of what a show can be, where things in outside nature appear as temptations just as they would in a saint's mind.

Theatre must rediscover its true meaning in this spectacle of a temptation, where life stands to lose everything and the mind to gain everything.

Besides, we have put forwards a programme which permits pure production methods discovered on the spot to be organized around historic or cosmic themes familiar to all.

And we insist that the first Theatre of Cruelty show will hinge on these mass concerns, more urgent and disturbing than any personal ones.

We must find out whether sufficient production means, financial or otherwise, can be found in Paris, before the cataclysm occurs, to allow such theatre (which must remain because it is the future) to come to life. Or whether real blood is needed right now to reveal this cruelty.

May 1933

The Theatre of Cruelty*
First Manifesto

We cannot continue to prostitute the idea of theatre whose only value lies in its agonizing magic relationship to reality and danger.*

Put in this way, the problem of theatre must arouse universal attention, it being understood that theatre, through its physical aspect and because it requires *spatial expression* (the only real one in fact) allows the sum total of the magic means in the arts and words to be organically active like renewed exorcisms. From the foregoing it becomes apparent that theatre will never recover its own specific powers of action until it has also recovered its own language.

That is, instead of harking back to texts regarded as sacred and definitive, we must first break theatre's subjugation to the text and rediscover the idea of a kind of unique language somewhere in between gesture and thought.

We can only define this language as expressive, dynamic spatial potential in contrast with expressive spoken-dialogue potential. Theatre can still derive possibilities for extension from speech outside words, the development in space of its dissociatory, vibratory action on our sensibility. We must take inflection into account here, the particular way a word is pronounced, as well as the visual language of things (audible, sound language aside), also movement, attitudes and gestures, providing their meanings are extended, their features connected even as far as those signs, making a kind of alphabet out of those signs. Having become conscious of this spatial language, theatre owes it to itself to organize these shouts, sounds, lights and onomatopoeic language, creating true hieroglyphs out of characters and objects, making use of their symbolism and interconnections in relation to every organ and on all levels.

Therefore we must create word, gesture and expressive metaphysics, in order to rescue theatre from its human, psychological prostration. But all this is of no use unless a kind of real metaphysical temptation, invoking certain unusual notions, lies behind such an effort, for the latter by their

63

very nature cannot be restricted or even formally depicted. These ideas on Creation, Growth and Chaos are all of a cosmic order, giving us an initial idea of a field now completely alien to theatre. They can create a kind of thrilling equation between Man, Society, Nature and Objects.

Anyhow, there is no question of putting metaphysical ideas directly on stage but of creating kinds of temptations, vacuums, around these ideas. Humour and its anarchy, poetry and its symbolism and imagery, give us a kind of primary idea of how to channel the temptation in these ideas.

Here we ought to mention the purely physical side of this language, that is to say all the ways and means it has of acting on our sensibility.

It would be futile to say it calls on music, dancing, mime or mimicry. Obviously it uses moves, harmonies, rhythms, but only up to the point where they can cooperate in a kind of pivotal expression without favouring any particular art. However, this does not mean it omits ordinary facts and emotions, but it uses them as a springboard in the same way as HUMOUR as DESTRUCTION can serve to reconcile laughter with our reasoning habits.

But this tangible, objective theatre language captivates and bewitches our senses by using a truly oriental concept of expression. It runs through our sensibility. Abandoning our Western ideas of speech, it turns words into incantation. It expands the voice. It uses vocal vibrations and qualities, wildly trampling them underfoot. It piledrives sounds. It aims to exalt, to benumb, to bewitch, to arrest our sensibility. It liberates a new lyricism of gestures which, because it is distilled and spatially amplified, ends by surpassing the lyricism of words. Finally it breaks away from language's intellectual subjugation by conveying the sense of a new, deeper intellectualism hidden under these gestures and signs and raised to the dignity of special exorcisms.

For all this magnetism, all this poetry, all these immediately bewitching means would be to no avail if they did not put the mind bodily on the track of something, if true theatre could not give us the sense of a creation where we are in possession of only one of its facets, while its completion exists on other levels.

And it makes no difference whether these other levels are really conquered by the mind, that is to say by our intellect, for this curtails them, a pointless and meaningless act. What matters is that our sensibility is put into a deeper, subtler state of perception by assured means, the very object of magic and ritual, of which theatre is only a reflection.

Technique

The problem is to turn theatre into a function in the proper sense of the word, something as exactly localized as the circulation of our blood through our veins, or the apparently chaotic evolution of dream images in the mind, by an effective mix, truly enslaving our attention.

Theatre will never be itself again, that is to say will never be able to form truly illusive means, unless it provides the audience with truthful distillations of dreams where its taste for crime, its erotic obsessions, its savageness, its fantasies, its utopian sense of life and objects, even its cannibalism, do not gush out on an illusory make-believe but on an inner level.

In other words, theatre ought to pursue a re-examination not only of all aspects of an objective, descriptive outside world, but also all aspects of an inner world, that is to say man viewed metaphysically, by every means at its disposal. We believe that only in this way will we be able to talk about imagination's rights in the theatre once more. Neither Humour, Poetry nor Imagination mean anything unless they re-examine man organically through anarchic destruction, his ideas on reality and his poetic position in reality generating stupendous flights of forms constituting the whole show.

But to view theatre as a second-hand psychological or moral operation and to believe dreams themselves only serve as a substitute is to restrict both dreams' and theatre's deep poetic range. If theatre is as bloody and as inhuman as dreams, the reason for this is that it perpetuates the metaphysical notions in some Fables in a present-day, tangible manner, whose atrocity and energy are enough to prove their origins and intentions in fundamental first principles rather than to reveal and unforgettably tie down the idea of continual conflict within us, where life is continually lacerated, where everything in creation rises up and attacks our condition as created beings.

This being so, we can see that by its proximity to the first principles poetically infusing it with energy, this naked theatre language, a non-virtual but real language using man's nervous magnetism, must allow us to transgress the ordinary limits of art and words actively – that is to say, magically – to produce a kind of total creation *in real terms*, where man must reassume his position between dreams and events.

revised from start to finish. Fineness, density and opacity factors must be reintroduced into lighting, so as to produce special tonal properties, sensations of heat, cold, anger, fear and so on.

Costume: As to costume, without believing there can be any uniform stage costume that would be the same for all plays, modern dress will be avoided as much as possible, not because of a fetishistic superstition for the past, but because it is perfectly obvious certain age-old costumes of ritual intent, although they were once fashionable, retain a revealing beauty and appearance because of their closeness to the traditions which gave rise to them.

The Stage – The Auditorium: We intend to do away with stage and auditorium, replacing them with a kind of single, undivided locale without any partitions of any kind and this will become the very scene of the action. Direct contact will be established between the audience and the show, between actors and audience, from the very fact that the audience is seated in the centre of the action, is encircled and furrowed by it. This encirclement comes from the shape of the house itself.

Abandoning the architecture of present-day theatres, we will rent some kind of barn or hangar rebuilt along lines culminating in the architecture of some churches, holy places or certain Tibetan temples.

This building will have special interior height and depth dimensions. The auditorium will be enclosed within four walls stripped of any ornament, with the audience seated below, in the middle, on swivelling chairs allowing them to follow the show taking place around them. In effect, the lack of a stage in the normal sense of the word will permit the action to extend itself to the four corners of the auditorium. Special places will be set aside for the actors and action in the four cardinal points of the hall. Scenes will be acted in front of washed walls designed to absorb light. In addition, overhead galleries run right around the circumference of the room as in some Primitive paintings. These galleries will enable actors to pursue one another from one corner of the hall to the other as needed, and the action can extend in all directions at all perspective levels of height and depth. A shout could be transmitted by word of mouth from one end to the other with a succession of amplifications and inflections.

The action will unfold, extending its trajectory from floor to floor, from place to place, with sudden outbursts flaring up in different spots like conflagrations. And the show's truly illusive nature will not be empty words any more than the action's direct, immediate hold on the spectators. For the action, diffused over a vast area, will require the lighting for one scene and the varied lighting for a performance to hold the audience as well as the characters – and physical lighting methods, the thunder and wind whose repercussions will be experienced by the spectators, will correspond with several actions at once, several phases in one action with the characters clinging together like swarms, will endure all the onslaughts of the situations and the external assaults of weather and storms.

However, a central site will be retained which, without acting as a stage properly speaking, enables the body of the action to be concentrated and brought to a climax whenever necessary.

Objects – Masks – Props: Puppets, huge masks, objects of strange proportions appear by the same right as verbal imagery, stressing the physical aspect of all imagery and expression – with the corollary that all objects requiring a stereotyped physical representation will be discarded or disguised.

Decor: No decor. Hieroglyphic characters, ritual costume, thirty-foot-high effigies of King Lear's beard in the storm, musical instruments as tall as men, objects of unknown form and purpose are enough to fulfil this function.

Topicality: But, you may say, theatre so removed from life, facts or present-day activities... news and events, yes! Anxieties, whatever is profound about them, the prerogative of the few, no! In the *Zohar*, the story of the Rabbi Simeon* is as inflammatory as fire, as topical as fire.

Works: We will not act written plays, but will attempt to stage productions straight from subjects, facts or known works. The type and layout of the auditorium itself governs the show as no theme, however vast, is precluded to us.

Show: We must revive the concept of an integral show. The problem is to express it, spatially nourish and furnish it, like tap holes drilled into a flat wall of rock, suddenly generating geysers and bouquets of stone.

The Actor: The actor is both a prime factor, since the show's success depends on the effectiveness of his acting, as well as a kind of neutral, pliant factor, since he is rigorously denied any individual initiative. Besides, this is a field where there are no exact rules. And there is a wide margin dividing a man from an instrument, between an actor required to give nothing more than a certain number of sobs and one who has to deliver a speech, using his own powers of persuasion.*

Interpretation: The show will be coded from start to finish, like a language. Thus no moves will be wasted, all obeying a rhythm, every character being typified to the limit, each gesture, feature and costume to appear as so many shafts of light.

Cinema: Through poetry, theatre contrasts pictures of the unformulated with the crude visualization of what exists. Besides, from an action viewpoint, one cannot compare a cinema image, however poetic it may be, since it is restricted by the film, with a theatre image which obeys all life's requirements.

Cruelty: There can be no spectacle without an element of cruelty as the basis of every show. In our present degenerative state, metaphysics must be made to enter the mind through the body.

The Audience: First, this theatre must exist.

Programme: Disregarding the text, we intend to stage:

1. An adaptation of a Shakespearean work, absolutely consistent with our present confused state of mind, whether this be an apocryphal Shakespeare play such as *Arden of Faversham* or another play from that period.*

2. A very free poetic play by Léon-Paul Fargue.

3. An excerpt from *The Zohar*, the Story of Rabbi Simeon, which has the ever present force and virulence of a conflagration.

4. The story of Bluebeard, reconstructed from historical records, containing a new concept of cruelty and eroticism.

5. The Fall of Jerusalem, according to the Bible and the Scriptures. On the one hand a blood-red colour flowing from it, that feeling of running wild and mental panic visible even in daylight. On the other hand, the prophets' metaphysical quarrels, with the dreadful intellectual agitation they cause, their reaction rebounding bodily on the King, the Temple, the Masses and Events.

6. One of the Marquis de Sade's tales, its eroticism transposed, allegorically represented and cloaked in the sense of a violent externalization of cruelty, masking the remainder.*

7. One or more Romantic melodramas where the unbelievable will be an active, tangible, poetic factor.

8. Büchner's *Woyzeck** in a spirit of reaction against our principles, and as an example of what can be drawn from an exact text in terms of the stage.

9. Elizabethan theatre works stripped of the lines, retaining only their period machinery, situations, character and plot.*

Letters on Cruelty*

First Letter

Paris, 13th September 1932

To J.P.*

My Dear Friend,

I can give you no details about my Manifesto without spoiling its emphasis. All I can do for the time being is to make a few remarks to try and justify my choice of title, the Theatre of Cruelty.

This cruelty is not sadistic or bloody, at least not exclusively so.

I do not systematically cultivate horror. The word cruelty must be taken in its broadest sense, not in the physical, predatory sense usually ascribed to it. And in doing, I demand the right to make a break with its usual verbal meaning, to break the bonds once and for all, to break asunder the yoke, finally to return to the etymological origins of language, which always evoke a tangible idea through abstract concepts.

One may perfectly well envisage pure cruelty without any carnal laceration. Indeed, philosophically speaking, what is cruelty? From a mental viewpoint, cruelty means strictness, diligence, unrelenting decisiveness, irreversible and absolute determination.

From the aspect of our own existence, the most current philosophical determinism is an image of cruelty.

We are wrong to make cruelty mean merciless bloodshed, pointless pursuits unrelated to physical ills. The Ethiopian Ra, carting off defeated princes and imposing servitude on them, was not driven to do so by a desperate thirst for blood. In fact, cruelty is not synonymous with bloodshed, martyred flesh or crucified enemies. Associating cruelty and torture is only one minor aspect of the problem. Practising cruelty involves a higher determination to which the executioner-tormentor is also subject and which he must be *resolved* to endure when the time comes. Above all, cruelty is very lucid, a kind of strict control and submission to necessity. There is no cruelty without consciousness, without the application of consciousness, for the latter gives practising any act in life a blood-red tinge, its cruel overtones, since it is understood that being alive always means the death of someone else.

Second Letter

Paris, 14th November 1932

To J.P.

My Dear Friend,

Cruelty is not an adjunct to my thoughts, it has always been there, but I had to become conscious of it. I use the word cruelty in the sense of hungering after life, cosmic strictness, relentless necessity, in the Gnostic sense of a living vortex engulfing darkness, in the sense of the inescapably necessary pain without which life could not continue. Good has to be desired, it is the result of an act of will-power, while evil is continuous. When the hidden god creates, he obeys a cruel need for creation imposed on him, yet he cannot avoid creating, thus permitting an ever more condensed, ever more consumed nucleus of evil to enter the eye of the intentional vortex of good. Theatre in the sense of constant creation, a wholly magic act, obeys this necessity. A play without this desire, this blind zest for life, capable of surpassing everything seen in every gesture or every act, in the transcendent aspect of the plot, would be useless and a failure as theatre.

Third Letter

Paris, 16th November 1932

To Mr R. de R.*

My Dear Friend,

I confess I do not understand or accept the objections you raised against the title of my book. For it seems to me creation, life itself, can only be defined by a kind of strictness, the fundamental cruelty guiding things towards their inexorable goal, whatever the cost.

Effort means cruelty, existence through effort is cruel. Rising from his repose and straining himself towards being, Brahma suffered, and this may perhaps convey joyful melodies, but at the limits of the curve it is only expressed as an awful crushing.

There is a form of incipient spitefulness in the flame of life, in love of life, life's irrational impulse. Erotic desire is cruel since it feeds on contingencies. Death is cruelty, resurrection is cruelty, transfiguration is cruelty, for true death has no place in all the meanings of an enclosed, circular world, ascension means rending, this enclosed space is nurtured by lives, each stronger life passes over the others, consuming them in slaughter, transfiguring good. In a world made manifest, where, metaphysically speaking, evil is the paramount rule, whatever is good is an effort, further cruelty superimposed on all other.

If one does not understand this, one does not understand metaphysical ideas. And after this let no one come and tell me the title of my book is too restricted. Cruelty connects things together, the different stages of creation are formed by it. Good is always an external façade, but the inner façade is evil. Evil will eventually be reduced, but only at the final moment, when all forms are on the point of returning to chaos.

Letters on Language

First Letter

Paris, 15th September 1931

To Mr B.C.*

Sir,

In an article on staging and theatre you stated: "One risks making a terrible mistake by considering staging as an autonomous art", and that: "Performance, the spectacular side of a dramatic work, cannot operate alone or make its own decisions completely independently."

You go on to add that these are elementary truths.

You are perfectly right to consider staging merely an auxiliary, minor art, so that even those who employ it with the maximum freedom deny it any fundamental originality. As long as staging remains just a means of presentation, a subordinate way of expressing works, a kind of display interlude without any meaning of its own even in the minds of the boldest producers, it has no value except insofar as it succeeds in hiding behind the works it is intended to serve. And this will continue as long as the principal interest in performed works lies in the script, as long as in theatre – a performing art – literature takes precedence over a kind of performance incorrectly called the show, with everything this term entails that is disparaging, subsidiary, ephemeral and external.

What seems to me a first truth above all else is this: in order for theatre, an independent autonomous art, to be revived, or simply to stay alive, it must clearly indicate what differentiates it from the script, from pure speech, literature and all other predetermined, written methods.

We might perfectly well go on considering theatre as based on the authority of the script, on a more and more wordy, diffuse and tiring script to which stage aesthetics would be subject.

But this concept consists in having characters sit on a number of chairs or couches placed in a row and tell each other stories, however wonderful these might be. And even if this is not a complete denial of theatre, which does not absolutely demand movement to be what it ought to be, it is certainly a distortion.

If theatre has become essentially psychological, the intellectual alchemy of feelings and the pinnacle of dramatic art has come to consist of a certain ideal silence and stillness, this is nothing else but a staged distortion of the idea of concentration.

For this concentrated acting, used among so many other expressive means by the Japanese, for example, is valuable only as one method among many. And to make this theatre's aim is to avoid using the stage; just like someone who, having the whole of the Pyramids in which to bury a Pharaoh's body, blows them up on the pretext that a niche will accommodate it just as well.

But at the same time he would have to blow up the magic, philosophical system of which the niche was only the starting point and the body only a condition.

On the other hand, a producer who takes pains over staging to the detriment of the lines is wrong, perhaps less wrong than a critic who accuses him of an exclusive concern with staging.

For a producer remains true to theatre tradition, which deals with staging by taking pains over staging, that is, over the truly specifically theatrical part of the show. But both these are playing on words, for if the term staging has assumed such a disparaging meaning, this is the fault of our European concept of theatre, making speech predominate over other means of performance.

No one has ever definitely proved word language is the best. And it seems that on stage, above all a space to be filled, somewhere something happens, word language must give way to sign language, whose objective aspect has the most immediate impact on us.

Viewed from this angle, the aim of stage work reassumes a kind of intellectual dignity, words effacing themselves behind gesture, and from the fact that the aesthetic, plastic part of theatre abandons its role as a decorative interlude, to become a *language* of direct communication in the proper sense of the word.

In other words, if it is true that in a play made to be spoken, the producer is wrong to become sidetracked on more or less intelligently lit scenic effects, group acting, muted moves, all of that which could be termed skin-deep effects that only overload the script, in so doing he is closer to theatre's tangible reality than an author who might have confined himself to books, without resorting to the stage, whose spatial requirements seemed to escape him.

One might object by pointing to the great dramatic value of all the great tragedians whose literary, or at least verbal side seems predominant.

My answer to this is that if we are so incapable today of giving any idea of Aeschylus, Sophocles or Shakespeare that is worthy of them, this is very likely because we have lost any idea of the natural philosophy of their theatre. Because all the immediately human, active aspects of delivery, gesture or stage rhythm escape us, and these ought to have as much if not more importance than the admirable spoken dissection of their heroes' psychology.

Through this aspect, through these exact gestures modified during the course of history and making feelings current, we can rediscover the deep humanity in their drama.

But even if this natural philosophy really existed, I would still maintain none of these great tragedians are theatre alone, which is a matter of stage embodiment, only coming alive by embodiment. Call theatre a minor art if you like – that remains to be seen! – but theatre consists of a certain manner of filling and animating stage space, by sparking off emotions, human feelings at a given point, creating ecstatic situations expressed in tangible gestures.

Furthermore, these tangible gestures must be sufficiently effective to make us forget the very need for dialogue. Yet if dialogue exists, it must do so as a response, a relay in activated space, and the mortar in these gestures must achieve the value of true abstraction through its human effectiveness.

In a word, theatre must become a kind of experimental manifestation of the deep-seated identity between the abstract and the concrete.

For a gesture culture also exists side by side with word culture. There are other languages in the world besides our Western languages which have decided in favour of despoiling and desiccating ideas, presenting them in an inert, stale manner, unable to stir up in their course a whole system of natural affinities, as do oriental languages.

It is only right that theatre should remain the most effective and active place where these tremendous kindred disturbances can pass through us, where ideas are arrested in flight at some point in their metamorphosis into the abstract.

No complete theatre can fail to take this gristly metamorphosis of ideas into account, which does not add the expression of states of mind belonging to the field of semi-consciousness to our known, ready-made feelings, which suggestive gestures will always convey more adequately than the definite, exact meaning of words.

Briefly, it seems the highest possible concept of theatre is one which philosophically reconciles us with Becoming and which, through all kinds of objective situations, suggests the covert notion of the passage and metamorphosis of ideas, far more than the shock of feelings transmuted into words.

It also seems theatre certainly arose from a desire of this kind, that man and his appetites must only obtrude to the degree that he is magnetically confronted with his fate. Not to submit to it, but to measure up to it.

Second Letter

Paris, 28th September 1932

To J.P.*

My Dear Friend,
Once you have read my Manifesto, I do not believe you could persist in your objections; either you have not read it, or read it badly. My shows have nothing to do with Copeau's improvisations.* However much they may be steeped in tangibles, in externals, however much they are rooted in outdoor nature and not in the mind's narrow cells, for all that they are not committed to the whims of an actor's rough-and-ready inspiration, especially modern actors, who once they step outside the text plunge blindly on. I would not care to entrust the fate of my shows and theatre to that kind of chance. No.

This is what will really happen. Nothing less than changing the starting point of artistic creation and upsetting theatre's customary rules. We must use nature's own distinctive language in place of speech, its expressive potential being equal to verbal language, while its source is taken at an even more buried and remote point in thought.

This new language's grammar is undiscovered as yet. Gesture is its substance and mind or, if you like, its alpha and omega. It springs from a NEED for speech rather than preformed speech. But finding a deadlock in speech, it spontaneously returns to gesture. On the way it touches on a few of the rules of substantial human expression. It is steeped in necessity. It poetically retraces the steps which culminated in the creation of language, but increasingly conscious of those worlds disturbed by word language which it brings to life in all their aspects. It brings to light the fixed incorporated relations in the strata of human syllables, which has killed them by confining them. It reconstructs all the processes by which words have come to mean that fiery Light-Bringer, whose Father Fire protects us like a shield, in the form of Jupiter, a Latin contraction for the Greek Zeus-Pater, all these processes by means of shouts, onomatopoeia, symbols, postures, or by slow, copious and emotional nervous inflections, stage by stage and term by term. For I submit words do not necessarily mean everything, either in essence or because of their predetermined nature, decided once and for all, they stop, they paralyse thought instead of fostering its development. By development I mean true, tangible, far-reaching qualities, since we live in a tangible, far-reaching world. Therefore this language aims at encompassing, using expansion, that is to say, space, and by using it, to make it speak out. I take objects, far-reaching things such as imagery and words, bring them together and make them respond to each other following the rules of symbolism and living analogy. Eternal laws, those of all poetry and viable language, among others, Chinese ideograms and ancient Egyptian hieroglyphs. Thus, far from restricting language and theatre potential, ostensibly because I will not perform written plays, I am extending stage language and increasing its potential.

I have added another language to speech and am attempting to restore its ancient magic effectiveness, its spellbinding effectiveness, integral to speech and whose mysterious potential is now forgotten. When I say I will not put on written plays, I mean I will not act plays based on writing or words, rather, in the shows I intend to put on, the predominant part will be physical and could not be determined or written in normal word language. Even the written or spoken parts will be performed in a different way.

Contrary to the practice here, that is to say in Europe or more correctly in the West, theatre will no longer be based on dialogue and the little dialogue remaining will not be written out, pre-arranged or determined a priori, but will be made up on stage, created on stage, correlating with the other language, with the required postures, symbols, moves and objects. But all this objective groping among one's material, where Words appear a necessity, resulting from a series of condensations, shocks, stage friction, all kinds of developments – (in this way theatre will become a genuine living operation, it will retain that kind of passionate pulsation without which art is pointless) – all this groping, all these experiments and jolts will nevertheless culminate in an *inscribed* composition, every last detail decided on and recorded by means of notation. Instead of taking place in an author's mind, this composition, this creation will take place in nature itself, in real space, and the final result will remain as meticulous and calculated as any written work, in addition to having enormous objective wealth.

PS: The author must assume what belongs to staging, as much as whatever belongs to the author must be restored to him, but he must become a producer himself so as to end the absurd dualism existing between author and producer.

An author who does not handle the stage material himself, does not evolve on stage by finding his way, by making the show follow the strength of his direction, has really betrayed his responsibilities. It is only right he should be replaced by actors, but so much the worse for theatre which is forced to undergo such an appropriation.

Theatre time, based on breathing, sometimes rushes out in a major, consciously willed exhalation, at other times contracts and attenuates to a prolonged feminine inhalation. An arrested gesture causes a frantic, complex teeming, and this gesture contains the magic of its evocation.

But if we enjoy providing suggestions concerning theatre's dynamic, animated life, we would not want to establish any rules.

Human breathing certainly obeys rules which are founded in all the innumerable combinations of the Cabalistic ternaries. There are six main ternaries, but numberless combinations, since all life stems from them. And theatre is precisely the place where this magic breathing is reproduced at will. If determining a significant gesture brings on sharp, rapid breathing around it, that same breathing's waves, if increased, can slowly break around a predetermined gesture. There are abstract principles, but no tangible, plastic rules. The only rule is poetic dynamism, proceeding from a strangled silence to the hurried sketch of a spasm or from individual speech *mezzo voce* to the heavy, resonant thunder of a gradually surging choir.

The main thing is to create stages, perspectives between one language and the other. Theatre's spatial secret lies in dissonance, tonal changes and expressive dialectic discontinuity.

Those who have some idea what language is will be able to understand us. We write for them alone. A few additional details, which complete the First Manifesto of the Theatre of Cruelty, are given below.

Everything vital having been said in the First Manifesto, the Second only aims at elaborating a few points. It provides a workable definition of Cruelty and suggests a description of stage space. It remains to be seen what we make of it.

Third Letter

Paris, 9th November 1932

To J.P.

My Dear Friend,

Those objections made both to you and me against my Theatre of Cruelty Manifesto first of all involve cruelty, whose function in my theatre seems unclear at least as an essential, decisive factor, and secondly involves theatre such as I see it.

As to the first objection, I would say those who raised it were correct, not in relation to cruelty or theatre, but in relation to the position this cruelty occupies in my theatre. I ought to have defined the very special way I used the word, for as I have said, I was not using it in a discursive, subordinate sense, or out of a taste for sadistic mental perversion, a love for extraordinary feelings or unhealthy attitudes, therefore not at all in an incidental way. It is not a matter of vicious cruelty, cruelty proliferating with perverted desires, expressed in bloody acts, sickly excrescences on already polluted flesh, but on the contrary a pure, unworldly feeling, a true mental process modelled on the gestures of life itself, the idea being that because life, metaphysically speaking, accepts range, depth, weight and matter, it accepts evil in direct consequence and everything inherent in evil, namely space, range and matter. All of which culminates in consciousness and anguish, and consciousness in anguish. Life cannot fail to exercise the blind severity all these contingencies bring or else it would not be life. But cruelty is this severity and this life which exceeds all bounds and is practised in torture, trampling everything down, that pure inexorable feeling.

Therefore I said "cruelty" just as I might have said "life" or "necessity", because I wanted especially to denote that theatre to me means continual action and emergence, above all there is nothing static about it, I associate it with a true act, therefore alive, therefore magic.

And I am searching for all the technical and empirical ways of bringing theatre closer to the loftier, maybe excessive, at any rate living and turbulent ideas I have of theatre.

As to the Manifesto's arrangement, I must admit it is uneven and largely a failure.

I have suggested exact, unexpected rules of grim and terrifying aspect, and the moment one expects me to justify them, I go on to the next principle.

The Manifesto's dialectic is admittedly weak. I jumped from one idea to the next without any progression. No inner need can justify its layout.

As to the second principal objection, I claim the producer, having become a kind of demiurge with this idea of inexorable pureness always in the back of his mind, to achieve it at any cost if he really wants to be a producer, therefore a man versed in the nature of matter and objects, must pursue his exploration of intense movement in the physical field and exact affective gestures which are the equivalent of the most absolute and complete moral discipline in the psychological field. Unleashing certain blind forces on a cosmic level, activating whatever they must activate, pulverizing and burning whatever they must pulverize and burn on the way.

The following are my overall conclusions:

Theatre is no longer an art, or it is a useless art. It conforms at every point to our Western concepts of art. We are overloaded with ineffectual, decorative feelings, aimless activity devoted solely to entertainment and the picturesque. We want active theatre, but on a level as yet undefined.

We need true action without any practical results. Theatre action does not unfold on a social level, still less on ethical or psychological levels.

Clearly this is not a simple problem. But however disordered, incomprehensible and repetitive the Manifesto may be, at least it does not evade the real issue, rather it tackles it head on, which no one in the theatre had dared to do for many years. Up to now no one had tackled the principle of theatre itself, which is metaphysical, and if there have been so few worthwhile plays it is not for lack of talent or playwrights.

The question of talent aside, there is a basic error of principle in European theatre. This mistake is tied up with the whole system of things where absence of talent appears as a result and not just a simple accident.

If the times have turned aside from and lost interest in theatre, the reason is that theatre does not represent them any more. They no longer wait for it to provide them with Myths on which they might sustain themselves.

We probably live in a unique period of history where a riddled world sees its old values crumbling away. If the foundations of burnt-up life dissolve, on an ethical and social level this is expressed in a monstrous unleashing of lust unbridling the basest instincts, and the crackling of burnt-out lives prematurely exposed to the flame.

The interesting thing about present-day events is not the events themselves, but this state of intellectual turmoil into which minds are plunged, this extreme tension, for they unendingly plunge us into a state of conscious confusion.

That all this disturbs the mind without making it lose its balance is a moving way of expressing the innate pulse of life.

Well, if theatre has turned away from a moving, legendary present, no wonder audiences have turned away from theatre that ignores the present to such an extent.

Thus we may reproach theatre, such as it is practised, with a terrible lack of imagination. Theatre must be on a par with life, not personal life, that side of life where CHARACTER reigns supreme, but a kind of emancipated life, sweeping human personality aside, where man is only a shadow. Theatre's true purpose is to create Myths, to express life from an immense, universal aspect and to deduce imagery from this life where we would like to discover ourselves.

And in so doing, to arrive at such a powerful kind of overall likeness it has an immediate effect.

May it free us with a Myth in which we have sacrificed our petty human personality, just like Characters from the Past, with powers rediscovered in the Past.

Fourth Letter

Paris, 28th May, 1933

To J.P.

My Dear Friend,

I did not say I wanted to exert any direct effect on our times; I said that the theatre I wanted to create, in order to be possible, to exist and be accepted by the times, presupposed another form of civilization.

Without representing its period, theatre can lead to a profound change in ideas, customs, beliefs and principles on which the spirit of the times are based. In any case that would not prevent me from doing what I want and doing it exactly. I intend to do what I have hoped to do or nothing at all.

As to the show itself, I cannot give you any further details, for two reasons:

1. For once, what I want to do is easier to do than to talk about.

2. I do not want to risk being plagiarized as has happened to me several times in the past.

I believe no one has the right to call themselves authors, that is to say creators, except those who control the management of the stage directly. And this is precisely theatre's weak point, such as it is viewed not only in France, but in Europe and even throughout the whole of the West. Western theatre acknowledges spoken language as the only language, that is, only ascribes the properties and qualities of a language, only permits it to be called language, with the kind of intellectual merit generally ascribed to that word when it is grammatically spoken, that is to say word language, written words, having no greater value whether spoken or merely written.

In theatre such as we conceive it here, the script is everything. It is understood that word language is the major language, it is definitely accepted, has become a part of our customs and mentality and has an established intellectual value. Yet even from a Western point of view we must agree words have become fossilized, words, all words are frozen, straitjacketed by their meanings, within restricted, diagrammatized terminology. Written words have as much value in theatre as it is performed here as the same words spoken, which lead some theatre lovers to say that to read a play affords them just as express and great pleasure as seeing the same play performed. Everything relating to the particular enunciation of a word escapes them, the vibration it can set up in space, and in consequence everything it can add to thought. A word thus understood has only little more than an indirect, that is to say a clarificatory, meaning. Under these conditions it is no exaggeration to say that in view of their clearly defined, limited terminology, words are made to stop thought, to surround it, to complete it – in short they are only a conclusion.

Obviously poetry did not abandon theatre without good reason. The fact that poetic playwrights have ceased to produce for so many years is not just an accident. Word language has its own rules. For the last four hundred and more years, especially in France, we have grown too used to employing words in theatre in a single, definite sense. We have made action revolve too exclusively around psychological subjects whose variations are not countless, far from it. Theatre has become overaccustomed to a lack of inquisitiveness and, above all, imagination.

Theatre, like speech, needs to be emancipated.

To persist in making characters converse about feelings, emotions, desires and impulses of a strictly psychological order, where one word is substituted for untold mimesis (since we are dealing with precision), such obstinacy caused theatre to lose any true reason for existing, and we have come to long for silence, in which we could listen more closely to life. Western psychology is expressed in dialogue, and an obsession with clearly defined words that say everything ends in words drying up.

Oriental theatre has been able to retain certain expansive values in words, since clear verbal meaning is not everything, for there is also the music of words, addressing itself directly to the subconscious. Thus there is no spoken language in oriental theatre, only a language of gestures, postures and symbols which, from the viewpoint of thought in action, has as much expansive and revelatory power as any other. And in the Orient this sign language is valued more than the other, ascribing direct, magic powers to it. It is called on to address not only the mind but also the senses, and through the senses to reach even richer and more fruitful areas of sensibility in full flight.

Thus if an author organizes word language and a producer is his servant, this is merely a matter of words. There is a confusion in terminology arising from the meaning usually ascribed to the term producer; for us he is only a craftsman, an adaptor, a kind of translator forever dedicated to making stage plays pass from one language to another. This confusion will only be possible and the producer will only be required to take a back seat to the author as long as it remains understood that word language is superior to all others and that theatre allows no other.

But if we were to return, however little, to the active, inspired, plastic wellsprings of language, reuniting words with the physical moves from which they originated, the logical discursive side of words would disappear beneath their physical, affective side, that is to say, instead of words being taken solely for what they mean grammatically, they would be understood from a sound angle or discerned in movements, these movements themselves being associated with other simple, direct movements as occur in many circumstances in life but not sufficiently with actor on stage. Then this literary language is reconstituted, comes alive, and besides, the objects themselves also begin to speak, just as they do in some Old Masters' canvases. Lighting, instead of acting as decor, assumes the appearance of an actual language and the objects on stage all vibrate with meaning, assume order, reveal figures. This direct, physical language is entirely at the producer's command, and this is his chance to build up a kind of absolute autonomy.

It would be strange if the person who controlled a field closer to life than any other, that is, the producer, had at all times to give way to the playwright who works essentially in the abstract, that is, on paper. Even if production did not have a language of gestures to its credit, equal to or even transcending words, any production with its moves, its numerous characters, lighting and decor could rival what is most profound in paintings such as Lucas van Leyden's *Lot and his Daughters*, certain of Goya's *Sabbaths*, some of El Greco's *Resurrections* and *Transfigurations*, Hieronymus Bosch's *The Temptation of St Anthony*, or that mysterious and disturbing *Dulle Griet* by Brueghel the Elder, where torrid red light, although localized in certain parts of the canvas, seems to well up on all sides and, through some technical process or other, arrests the viewer's mesmerized gaze several feet away from the painting, the whole teeming with theatre. The turmoil of life confined within a circle of white light suddenly run aground on nameless shallows. A ghastly screeching noise rises from this larval orgy, but bruised human skin can never approach the same colour. Real life is moving and white, hidden life is ghastly and immobile, having all the possible attitudes of numberless immobility. This silent theatre is far more expressive than if it had been given another language with which to express itself. Each of these paintings has a double sense, and aside from their purely pictorial aspect, they disclose a message revealing mysterious or terrible aspects of nature and the mind.

Luckily for theatre, however, production is much more than that. For besides performance and its dense, substantial means, pure production contains gesture, facial expressions and mobile attitudes, the tangible use of music, everything words contain as well as having words at its disposal. Rhythmic, syllabic repetition, special vocal inflection embracing the exact meaning of words, all arouse a greater number of mental images in the mind, producing a more or less hallucinatory state, obliging our sensibility and our minds to undergo a kind of anatomical deterioration which contributes to eliminating the pointlessness ordinarily distinguishing written poetry, for the whole problem of theatre revolves around this pointlessness.

The Theatre of Cruelty*
Second Manifesto

Whether they admit it or not, whether a conscious or unconscious act, at heart audiences are searching for a poetic state of mind, a transcendent condition by means of love, crime, drugs, war or insurrection.

The Theatre of Cruelty was created in order to restore an impassioned, convulsive concept of life to theatre, and we ought to accept the cruelty on which this is based in the sense of drastic strictness, the extreme concentration of stage elements.

This cruelty will be bloody if need be, but not systematically so, and will therefore merge with the idea of a kind of severe mental purity, not afraid to pay the cost one must pay in life.

1. Inner Meaning

That is to say, the subjects and themes dealt with.

The Theatre of Cruelty will choose themes and subjects corresponding to the agitation and unrest of our times.

It does not intend to leave the task of revealing man or life's contemporary Myths to the cinema. But it will do so in its own way, that is to say, contrary to the world slipping into an economic, utilitarian and technological state, it will bring major considerations and fundamental emotions back into style, since modern theatre has overlaid these with the veneer of pseudo-civilized man.

These themes will be universal, cosmic, performed according to the most ancient texts taken from Mexican, Hindu, Judaic and Iranian cosmogonies, among others.

Repudiating psychological man with his clear-cut personality and feelings, it will appeal to the whole man, not social man submissive to the law, warped by religions and precepts.

And both the upper and lower strata of the mind will play their part. The reality of the imagination and dreams will appear on a par with life.

In addition, great social upheavals, clashes between peoples, natural forces, the interventions of chance, the attractions of fate will all appear either directly in the movements and gestures of the characters elevated in stature like gods, heroes or monsters of legendary size, or else directly in material form obtained by new scientific processes.

These gods or heroes, these monsters, these natural, cosmic forces will be depicted according to pictures in the most venerable holy books or ancient cosmogonies.

2. Form

Furthermore, theatre's need to steep itself in the wellsprings of infinitely stirring and sensitive poetry, to reach the furthest removed, the most backward and inattentive part of the audience, achieved by a return to ancient primal Myths, not through the script but the production, will not be solely required to incarnate and particularly to bring these ancient conflicts *up to date*. That is to say, the themes will be transferred straight onto the stage but incarnated in moves, expressions and gestures, before gushing out in words.

In this way we can repudiate theatre's superstition concerning the script and the author's autocracy.

In this way also we will link up with popular, primal theatre sensed and experienced directly by the mind, without language's distortions and the pitfalls in speech and words.

Above all, we intend to base theatre on the show and we will bring a new concept of space into the show; all possible levels, all possible height and depth sight lines must be used, and a special notion of time coupled with movement will exist within this concept.

In addition to the greatest possible number of moves in a given time, the greatest possible amount of physical imagery and meaning must be combined with these moves.

The moves and imagery used will not exist solely to please eye and ear, but more profitably to please the intimate self, the mind.

Thus stage space will not only be measured by size or volume but from what one might term *a mysterious aspect*.

The overlapping of imagery and moves must culminate in a genuine physical language, no longer based on words but on signs formed through the combination of objects, silence, shouts and rhythms.

For it must be understood, we intend to introduce silence and rhythm into the great number of moves and images arranged within a given time as well as a certain physical pulsation and excitement, composed of really created, really used objects and gestures. One could say the spirit of the most ancient hieroglyphics will govern the creation of this pure stage language.

All popular audiences have always been fond of direct expression and imagery; spoken words and explicit verbal expression occur in all the clearest and most distinctly elucidated parts of the plot, those parts where life is lulled to sleep and consciousness takes over.

And words will be construed in an incantatory, truly magical sense, side by side with this logical sense – not only for their meaning, but for their forms, their sensual radiation.

For the actual appearance of these monsters, orgies of heroes and gods, a plastic revelation of powers, explosive interjections of poetry and humour, whose task is to disorganize and pulverize appearances in accordance with the analogous, anarchic principle of all true poetry, and only possess true magic in a hypnotically suggestive mood where the mind is affected by direct sensual pressure.

If the nerves, that is to say a certain physiological sensitivity, are deliberately omitted from today's after-dinner theatre, or left to the spectator's personal interpretation, the Theatre of Cruelty intends to return to all the tried-and-tested magic means of affecting sensitivity.

These means, consisting of differing intensities of colour, light or sound, using vibrations and tremors, musical, rhythmic repetition or the repetition of spoken phrases, bringing tonality or a general diffusion of light into play, can only achieve their full effect by using *discords*.

But instead of restricting these discords to dominating one sense alone, we mean to make them overlap from one sense to another, from colour to sound, words to lighting, tremoring gestures to tonality soaring with sound, and so on.

By eliminating the stage, shows made up and constructed in this manner will extend over the whole auditorium and will scale the walls from the ground up along slender catwalks, physically enveloping the audience, constantly immersing them in light, imagery, movements and sound. The set will consist of the characters themselves, grown as tall as gigantic puppets, landscapes of moving lights playing on objects or continually shifting masks.

And just as there are to be no empty spatial areas, there must be no let-up, no vacuum in the audience's mind or sensitivity. That is to say there will be no distinct divisions, no gap between life and theatre. Anyone who has watched a scene of any film being shot will understand just what I mean.

We want to have the same material means, lighting, extras and resources at our disposal for a stage show, as are daily squandered on reels of film, where everything that is active and magic about such a display is lost for ever.

* * *

The first Theatre of Cruelty show will be entitled:

THE CONQUEST OF MEXICO

This will stage events rather than men. Men will appear in their proper place with their emotions and psychology interpreted as the emergence of certain powers in the light of the events and historical destiny in which they played their role.

The subject was chosen:

1. Because it involves the present, and because of all the references it allows to problems of vital interest both to Europe and the world.

From a historical point of view, *The Conquest of Mexico* raises the question of colonization. It revives Europe's deep-rooted self-conceit in a burning, inexorably bloody manner, allowing us to debunk its own concept of its supremacy. It contrasts Christianity with far older religions. It treats the false conceptions the West has somehow formed concerning paganism and other natural religions with the contempt they deserve, emphasizing with burning emotion the splendour and ever present poetry of the ancient metaphysical foundations on which these religions were built.

2. By raising the dreadfully contemporary problem of colonization, that is, the right one continent considers it has to enslave another, it questions the real supremacy some races may have over others, showing the inner filiation linking a race's genius with particular forms of

civilization. It contrasts the tyrannical anarchy of the colonizers with the deep intellectual concord of those about to be colonized.

Further, by comparison with the European monarchical chaos at that time, based on the most unjust and dull-witted materialistic principles, it sheds light on the organic hierarchy of the Aztec monarchy established on indisputable spiritual principles.

From a social point of view, it demonstrates the peacefulness of a society which knew how to feed all its members and where the Revolution had taken place at its inception.

From the clash between the mental chaos in Catholic anarchy and pagan order, this subject can set off unbelievable holocausts of power and imagery, interspersed here and there with abrupt dialogue, hand-to-hand combat between men bearing the most opposed ideas within them like stigmata.

The inner mental meaning and the current interest in such a show having been sufficiently emphasized, we intend to highlight the *spectacular* merit of the conflicts it will stage.

First there is Montezuma's inner struggle, a king torn in two, history having been unable to enlighten us on his motives.

We will show his inner struggle, and his symbolic discussion with visualized astronomical myths in a pictorial, objective manner.

Finally, aside from Montezuma, there are the masses, the different social strata; the masses rising up against fate represented by Montezuma, the clamouring of the sceptics, quibbling philosophers and priests, the lamentations of the poets, middle-class and merchant treachery, the duplicity and sexual listlessness of the women.

The mentality of the masses, the spirit of events, will travel over the show in material waves, determining certain lines of force, and the diminished, rebelled or despairing consciousness of individuals will be carried along like straws.

Theatrically, the problem is to determine and harmonize these lines of force, to focus them and to obtain suggestive melodies from them.

These images, moves, dances, rituals, music, melodies cut short and sudden turns of dialogue will all be carefully recorded and described as far as one can in words, especially in the non-speaking parts of the show, the rule being to succeed in recording or codifying anything that cannot be described in words, just like in a musical score.

An Affective Athleticism

One must grant the actor a kind of affective musculature matching the bodily localization of our feelings.

An actor is like a physical athlete, with this astonishing corollary; his affective organism is similar to the athlete's, being parallel to it like a double, although they do not act on the same level.

The actor is a heart athlete.

In his case the whole man is also separated into three worlds; the affective area is his own.

It belongs to him organically.

The muscular movements of physical exertion are a likeness, a double of another exertion, located in the same points as stage-acting movements.

The actor relies on the same pressure points an athlete relies on to run, in order to hurl a convulsive curse whose course is driven inwards.

Similar anatomical bases can be found in all the feints in boxing, all-in wrestling, the hundred metres, the high jump and the movements of the emotions, since they all have the same physical support points.

With this further rider that the moves are reversed and in anything to do with breathing, for instance, an actor's body relies on breathing, while with a wrestler, a physical athlete, the breathing relies on his body.

The question of breathing is of prime importance; it is inversely proportional to external expression.

The more inward and restrained the expression, the more ample, concentrated and substantial breathing becomes, full of resonances.

Whereas breathing is compressed in short waves for ample, fiery externalized acting.

We can be sure that every mental movement, every feeling, every leap in human affectivity has an appropriate breath.

These breathing *tempi* have a name taught us by the cabbala, for they form the human heart and the gender of our emotional activity.

An actor is merely a crude empiricist, a practitioner guided by vague instinct.

Yet on no consideration does this mean we should teach him to rave.

What is at stake is to end this kind of wild ignorance in the midst of which all moves in present theatre are constantly faltering, as if through a haze. A gifted actor instinctively knows how to tap and radiate certain powers. But he would be astonished if he were told those powers which make their own substantial journey *through the senses* existed, for he never realized they could actually exist.

To use his emotions in the same way as a boxer uses his muscles, he must consider a human being as a Double, like the Kha of the Egyptian mummies, like an eternal ghost radiating affective powers.

As a supple, never-ending apparition, a form aped by the true actor, imposing the forms and picture of his own sensibility on it.

Theatre has an effect on this Double, this ghostly effigy it moulds, and like all ghosts this apparition has a long memory. The heart's memory endures and an actor certainly thinks with his heart, for his heart holds sway.

This means that in theatre more than anywhere else, an actor must become conscious of the emotional world, not by attributing imaginary merits to it, but those with concrete meaning.

Whether this hypothesis is exact or not, the main thing is that it can be authenticated.

The soul can be physiologically summarized as a maze of vibrations.

This ghostly soul can be regarded as exhilarated by its own cries, otherwise what are the Hindu mantras, those consonances, those strange stresses where the soul's secret side is hounded down into its innermost lairs, to reveal its secrets publicly.

Belief in the soul's flowing substantiality is essential to the actor's craft. To know that an emotion is substantial, subject to the plastic vicissitudes of matter, gives him control over his passions, extending our sovereign command.

To arrive at the emotions through their powers instead of regarding them as pure extraction, confers a mastery on an actor equal to a true healer's.

To know there is a physical outlet for the soul permits him to journey down into that soul in a reverse direction as well as to discover existence by calculated analogies.

To understand the mystery of passionate *time*, a kind of musical *tempo* conducting its harmonic beat, is an aspect of the drama modern psychological theatre has certainly disregarded for some time.

Now this *tempo* can be rediscovered analogically; it is to be found in the six ways of distributing and conserving breath as if it were a precious element.

All breathing has three measures, just as there are three basic principles in all creation, and the figures that correspond to them can be found in breathing itself.

The cabbala divides human breathing into six main arcana, the first, called the Great Arcanum, is creation:

ANDROGYNOUS	MALE	FEMALE
BALANCED	EXPANDING	ATTRACTING
NEUTER	POSITIVE	NEGATIVE

Therefore I thought of using a science of types of breathing, not only for an actor's work, but also in preparing him for his craft. For if a science of breathing sheds light on the tenor of the soul, it can stimulate the soul all the more by aiding it to flourish.

We can be sure that since breathing accompanies exertion, automatically produced breathing will give rise to a corresponding quality of exertion in the straining anatomy.

The exertion will have the tenor and rhythm of this artificially produced breathing.

Exertion sympathetically accompanies breathing, and according to the quality of the exertion to be produced, a preparatory projection of breathing will make this exertion easy and spontaneous. I stress the word "spontaneous", since breathing revives life, infusing fire into its matter.

This voluntary breathing incites the spontaneous reappearance of life. Like a many-coloured voice, warriors are sleeping at its edges. Matins or trumpet calls make them hurl themselves in ranks into the fray. But if a child suddenly cries "wolf", those same warriors awaken. Waken in the dead of night. False alarm; the soldiers are returning. No, they run into enemy units, falling into a real hornet's nest. The child cried out in his dreams. His supersensitive, hovering subconscious had run into a band of enemies. Thus in roundabout ways, fiction provoked by the drama lights on a reality deadlier than the former and unsuspected by life.

Thus an actor delves down into his personality by the whetted edge of his breathing.

For breathing which maintains life allows us to climb its stages step by step. If an actor does not have a certain feeling, he can probe it again through breathing, on the condition that he judiciously combines its effects, without mistaking its gender. For breathing is either male or female, less often bisexual. One may even have to portray some rare, fixed condition.

Breathing accompanies feeling, and the actor can penetrate this feeling through breathing, provided he knows how to distinguish which breathing suits which feeling.

As indicated above, there are six main breathing combinations:

NEUTER	MASCULINE	FEMININE
NEUTER	FEMININE	MASCULINE
MASCULINE	NEUTER	FEMININE
FEMININE	NEUTER	MASCULINE
MASCULINE	FEMININE	NEUTER
FEMININE	MASCULINE	NEUTER

And a seventh state higher than breathing, uniting the revealed and the unrevealed through the portals of a higher guna, the state of sattva.*

Should someone maintain an actor is not essentially a metaphysician and that this seventh state does not concern him, our answer is that if theatre is the most perfect and complete symbol of universal revelation, an actor bears the principle of this seventh state within him, this bloody artery along which he probes all the others, every time his controlled organs wake from their slumbers.

Surely instinct is there most of the time to make up for this absence of an indefinable idea. No need to fall as low as the ordinary emotions which fill current theatre. Moreover this breathing method was not devised for ordinary emotions. And rehearsed, cultivated breathing, following a method often used, was not made merely to prepare us for a declaration of adulterous love.

When an exhalation is rehearsed seven or twelve times it prepares us for the subtle quality of an outcry, for desperate soul demands.

We localize this breathing, distributing it between contracted and decontracted states. We use our bodies like screens through which will-power and relinquished will-power pass.

The tempo of voluntary thought makes us powerfully project a male beat, followed by a prolonged feminine beat without too apparent a transition.

The tempo of involuntary thought or even no thought at all and exhausted feminine breathing makes us inhale suffocating cellar heat, a monsoon wind, and on the same prolonged beat we exhale heavily. Yet throughout our whole body quivering by areas, our muscles never stopped functioning.

The main thing is to become conscious of these localizations of affective thought. One way of recognizing them is by exertion. The same pressure points which support physical exertion are also used in the emergence of affective thought. The same also act as a jumping-off point for the emergence of a feeling.

We ought to note that everything feminine, everything which is surrender, anguish, a plea, an invocation, stretching out towards something in a gesture of supplication, also rests on exertion pressure points, only like a diver who touches the seabed to rise to the surface. A kind of vacuum ray remains where the tension had been.

But in this case the masculine returns to haunt the feminine's place like a shadow. Whereas when the affective condition is male, the interior body consists of a kind of inverted geometry, a picture of the condition reversed.

To become conscious of physical obsession, muscles brushed by emotion, amounts to unleashing that emotion powerfully, and just as in active breathing, gives it secret, deep, unusually violent volume.

From the above it seems clear that any actor, even the least gifted, can increase the inner density and amplitude of his feelings through this physical science, and that a fuller expression follows this organic assumption.

It would do no harm for our purposes to become familiar with a few localized points.

Weightlifters lift with their backs, arching their backs to support the additional strength in their arms. And curiously enough, one inversely ascertains that every feminine draining feeling – sobs, sorrow, fitful pouting, fright – all this vacuum occurs in the small of the back, the very spot where Chinese acupuncture relieves congested kidneys. For Chinese medicine operates only according to fullness and emptiness. Convex and concave. Tense or relaxed. *Yin and Yang*. Masculine and Feminine.

There is another radiating pressure point: anger, bite and attack are located in the centre of the solar plexus. The brain relies on this point to eject its mental venom.

The point of heroism and the sublime is also that of guilt, where we strike our breasts, where anger boils up, raging but never advancing.

For wherever anger advances, guilt recedes; this is the secret of fullness and emptiness.

Acute, self-mutilating anger begins with a cracking neuter, becomes localized in the solar plexus by a swift feminine void, is clamped on both shoulder blades, then comes back like a boomerang, erupting sparks which burn themselves out without continuing. Although they lose their corrosive emphasis, they retain the correlation of male breathing and die out furiously.

I wanted to restrict myself to examples bearing on the few fertile principles comprising the material of this technical essay. Others, if they have time, can draw up the complete structure of the method. There are 380 points in Chinese acupuncture, with seventy-three major ones in normal therapy, but there are far fewer crude outlets for human emotions.

We can indicate far fewer pressure points on which to base the soul's athleticism.

The secret is to irritate those pressure points as if the muscles were flayed.

The rest is achieved by screams.

* * *

To reforge the links, the chain of a rhythm when audiences saw their own real lives in a show, we must allow audiences to identify with the show breath by breath and beat by beat.

It is not enough for the audience to be riveted by the show's magic and this will never happen unless we know where *to affect them*. We have had enough of chance magic or poetry which has no skill underlying it.

In theatre, poetry and skill must be associated as one from now on.

Every emotion has an organic basis and an actor changes his emotional voltage by developing his emotions within him.

The key to throwing the audience into a magical trance is to know in advance what pressure points must be affected in the body. But theatre poetry has long become unaccustomed to this invaluable kind of skill.

To be familiar with the points of localization in the body is to reforge the magic links.

Using breathing's hieroglyphics, I can rediscover a concept of divine theatre.

NB: In Europe no one knows how to scream any more, particularly actors in a trance no longer know how to cry out, since they do nothing but talk, having forgotten they have a body on stage, they have also lost the use of their throats. Abnormally shrunk, these throats are no longer organs but monstrous, talking abstractions. French actors now only know how to talk.

Two Notes

1. The Marx Brothers*

The first of the Marx Brothers' films we have seen here, *Animal Crackers*, seemed to me and to everybody *something extraordinary*, a special magic liberated by means of the screen, which normal relations between words and images do not usually reveal, and if there is a distinguishing state of mind, a distinct poetic mental level called *Surrealism*, *Animal Crackers* wholeheartedly shares in it.

It is difficult to say what this kind of magic consists of, in any case it may not even be anything specifically filmic, or even theatrical, and of which only a few successful Surrealist poems, *if they ever existed*, could give any idea. The poetic quality of a film like *Animal Crackers* could serve as a definition of humour, if the word had not long ago lost any meaning of complete freedom, the destruction of any mental reality.

In order to understand the powerful, utter, final, absolute (I am not exaggerating, I am simply trying to define and so much the worse if I get carried away in my enthusiasm) originality of a film such as *Animal Crackers* and at times (at least in the last part of the film) in *Monkey Business*, we ought to add to humour the idea of something tragic and disturbing, fatalism (neither happy nor unhappy but hard to express) which would slip in behind it like the revelation of a dreadful illness across a face of absolute beauty.

In *Monkey Business* we find the Marx Brothers, each with his own style, sure of themselves and ready, so we feel we come to grips with events. While in *Animal Crackers* each character loses face from the start, here, for three quarters of the film we watch the antics of clowns amusing themselves, making jokes, bringing some of them off very well, and the plot only thickens at the end when objects, animals, sounds, masters and servants, the host and his guests all go mad, everything runs wild and revolts amid the simultaneously entranced and lucid comments by one of the Marx Brothers, inspired by the spirit he has at last been able to unleash and of which he seems only a passing, amazed commentator. There is nothing at once so hallucinatory and terrible as this kind of manhunt, this battle between rivals, this chase in the darkness of a cattle barn, a stable draped with cobwebs, while men, women and animals stop the dance to land in the midst of a great pile of incongruous objects whose *movement* and *sound* are each used in turn.

In *Animal Crackers*, when a woman suddenly falls backwards onto a couch, her legs in the air, showing us for one moment everything we wanted to see, when a man abruptly throws himself on a woman in a parlour, dances a few steps with her, slapping her behind in time with the music, this is like the operation of a kind of intellectual freedom where each of the characters' subconscious, repressed by custom and usage, revenges itself and us at the same time. But when in *Monkey Business* a wanted man takes a lovely woman in his arms and dances with her *poetically*, with a kind of studied charm, striking graceful attitudes, the mental claims seem double, showing all that is poetic and perhaps even subversive in the Marx Brothers' jokes.

But the fact that the music the couple danced to, the wanted man and the lovely woman, is nostalgic, escapist music, *music of release*, gives enough indication of the dangerous side of all these jokes, for when the poetic mind acts, it is always inclined towards a kind of fiery anarchy, poetry's total disintegration of reality.

If Americans, since the spirit in this type of film is essentially their own, see only comedy in these films, and in comedy keep merely to the easy, funny limits of the word's meaning, so much the worse for them, but this cannot prevent us from considering the end of *Monkey Business* as a paean to anarchy and utter rebellion. A finale which places a calf's lowing on the same mental level as a woman's frightened cry, ascribing the same quality of lucid pain to it, that ending where, in the gloom of a dirty barn, two lecherous servants freely paw the naked shoulders of their master's daughter, treating the helpless master as equals, all this in the midst of the equally mental intoxication of the Marx Brothers' gyrations. The triumph of all this is both in the visual and oral exaltation all these events assume in the dark, in the pulsating level they attain and in the kind of powerful anxiety their concentration ultimately projects into the mind.

2. Around a Mother*
Dramatic Act by Jean-Louis Barrault

In Jean-Louis Barrault's show there is a kind of marvellous *centaur-horse*, and the thrill we felt at the sight of it was as great as if with the entrance of the *centaur-horse*, Jean-Louis Barrault had revived magic for us.

This show is magical in the same way as are the incantations of black witch doctors, when their tongues slapping their palates bring rain down on the land, when before the exhausted sick man, the witch doctor gives his breathing the form of a strange disease, driving out the sickness with his breath. Thus in Jean-Louis Barrault's show the moment the mother dies, a chorus of cries comes to life.

I do not know if such a success is a masterpiece, but in any case it is an event. When an atmosphere is so transformed that a hostile audience is suddenly and blindly immersed and invincibly disarmed, we must hail this as an event.

In this show there is a secret strength which wins the audience over, just as great love wins over a soul ripe for revolt.

Great, youthful love, youthful vigour, spontaneous, lively ebullience flows among the exact moves, the stylized, calculated gesticulation like the warbling of song birds through colonnades of trees in a magically arranged forest.

Here, in this religious atmosphere, Jean-Louis Barrault improvises a wild horse's movements, and we suddenly see he has turned into a horse.

His show proves the irresistible operations of gesture, it triumphantly demonstrates the importance of gesture and spatial movement. Stage perspective is restored to a position of importance it should never have lost. Finally he turns the stage into a living, moving place.

This show was organized in relation to the stage, *on* stage; it only comes alive on stage and there is not one point in stage perspective which does not assume a thrilling message.

There is a kind of immediate, physical aspect in this lively gesticulation, in the disjointed unfolding of figures, something as convincing as solace itself, which the memory will never forget.

Nor will one forget the mother's death, her spatial and temporal cries, the epic river crossing, anger rising in the hearts of men corresponding on a gestured level to the rising of another anger, especially that kind of man-horse weaving in and out of the play as if a Legendary spirit had come down among us.

Up to now only Balinese theatre seemed to have retained any trace of the latter spirit.

What difference does it make if Jean-Louis Barrault has revived a religious spirit by profane, descriptive means, if everything genuine is sacred, if the gestures are so fine they assume symbolic meaning?

Indeed, there are no symbols in Jean-Louis Barrault's play. And if we were to criticize his gestures at all, it is because they present a symbolic allusion while they ought to define reality. Thus, however fiery their action on us may be, it does not extend beyond itself.

It does not do so because it is merely descriptive, because it narrates external facts without any soul, because it does not touch either thoughts or souls on the raw, and it is here, rather than in the problem of knowing whether this is a theatrical form, that any criticism we may have of it can be made.

It uses theatrical means – for theatre which opens the physical field requires this field to be filled, for stage space to be furnished with gestures, for this space to be brought to life magically within itself, for an aviary of sounds to be unleashed and new relations found between sound, gestures and voices – we could say that what Jean-Louis Barrault has accomplished is theatre.

But on the other hand, this production does not share a theatrical state of mind, I mean deep drama, mystery deeper than souls, the lacerating conflict between souls where gesture is merely a course. Where man is only a point and lives drink at their source. But who has ever drunk at the sources of life?*

Notes

p. 1, *The Theatre and Its Double*: *The Theatre and Its Double* appeared in the Métamorphoses Collection (Gallimard) on 7th of February 1938. This work contains Antonin Artaud's collected essays on theatre dating from 1932; texts published in the *Nouvelle Revue Française*, lectures, manifestos and excerpts from letters.

Antonin Artaud considered collecting these texts into one volume in 1935, at the time when he wrote *The Cenci* and was looking for a theatre where he could stage this tragedy (see letter to Jean Paulhan dated 22nd February 1935). Once the performances of *The Cenci* at the Folies-Wagram had closed, Antonin Artaud had only one desire – to leave for Mexico. Before leaving he also wrote: *Oriental and Western Theatre*, *An Affective Athleticism*, *Seraphim's Theatre* and a note on Jean-Louis Barrault's production *Around a Mother*, all texts he wanted to add to the volume in preparation. On board ship bound for Mexico, he wrote to Jean Paulhan on 25th January 1936 that *he had found a suitable title for the book*; it was *The Theatre and Its Double*. On his return from Mexico and before plunging into the Irish escapade, Artaud corrected the proofs, but when *The Theatre and Its Double* appeared, he was confined in Saint-Anne mental hospital, near Rouen in Normandy.

p. 3, *Theatre and Culture*: There is no exact indication as to when this Preface was written. Although in the letters he wrote to Jean Paulhan about *The Theatre and Its Double*, both before leaving for Mexico and during his sojourn there, Antonin Artaud several times insisted that certain unpublished texts be included in the work, nowhere does he mention a preface. Likely it was written after the other texts. Besides, its subject matter proves it could only have been written after a study of Mexican civilization by Antonin Artaud. Yet he only wrote the first text devoted to Mexico, *The Conquest of Mexico*, in 1933. Later, after the failure of *The Cenci*, he decided to attempt his Mexican journey and then he began to study Mexican cosmogony and civilization seriously. At that time he may have considered writing a Preface (the three drafts and notes given in the Appendix seem to bear this out – Fragments I to VII seem to have been written before he left). But if this project had been completed, we can be sure there would be some indication of it when he made out a summary of *The Theatre and Its*

Double in a letter to Jean Paulhan dated 6th January 1936. Therefore it is not unlikely he wrote this text only after his return to Paris and added it to the final proofs.

p. 9, *Theatre and the Plague*: The text of a lecture given by Antonin Artaud at the Sorbonne on 6th April 1933. This text, published in the *Nouvelle Revue Française* (No. 253, 1st October 1934) underwent some changes when it was published in volume form.

p. 13, *Before any pronounced... coal-black dust*: It is likely Antonin Artaud took these notes from some medical treatise (Fragment IX in the Appendix) and they prove he wanted to give an exact clinical description of the plague.

p. 17, *Scipio*: Scipio Nasica, High Pontiff, who ordered that the theatres in Rome be razed to the ground and their cellars filled. (ARTAUD'S NOTE)

p. 23, *Production and Metaphysics*: Text of a lecture given by Antonin Artaud at the Sorbonne on 10th December 1932.

Antonin Artaud examined Lucas van Leyden's painting in the Louvre in September, 1931 and found similarities with Balinese theatre in it. Indeed, the original MS of this lecture is entitled *Painting*. The text was published in the *Nouvelle Revue Française* (No. 221, 1st February 1932).

p. 23, *Lucas van Leyden*: Lucas van Leyden (1494–1533), now known primarily as one of the greatest engravers of all time, was also one of the foremost painters of his age.

p. 23, *There is a work... from a distance*: Another version exists which differs slightly from the one given:

In the Louvre there is a painting by a Primitive artist, whether known or unknown I cannot say, but who in any case has remained unrecognized and whose name will certainly never be familiar to the masses, but who in my opinion cancels out the four or five centuries of painting that came after him, rendering them useless. This painter's name is Lucas van Leyden. He is a member of what art history textbooks call the Flemish Primitive School. I believe he died in 1453, although I could not vouch for the exactitude of this date, and he was born in 1413. The painting I am referring to uses a biblical subject in the style of the period, entitled *Lot and His Daughters*.

Today the Bible no longer inspires anyone, especially in the Arts, and we find any artist who was presumptuous enough to tackle a biblical subject both a bore and uninspired. Besides, our present-day understanding of the past is such, I mean made in such a manner, that to apply oneself to such a theme is a poor, lazy solution for someone searching for a fine subject.

Nevertheless the painting's strange pathos is evident at first sight, even from a distance.

p. 25, *several other details... eight-storey house*: If we compare Lucas van Leyden's painting and Antonin Artaud's description of it, we notice that many of the details he gives were reinvented by him. Everything occurs as if he were staging the subject anew.

p. 27, *those expressive means usable on stage*: Insofar as they show themselves able to profit by the direct physical potential offered by the stage, to replace the set forms of the art with living, threatening forms, through which the meaning of ancient ceremonial magic can find fresh reality on a theatrical level. Insofar as they accede to what one might call the *physical temptation* of the stage. (ARTAUD'S NOTE)

p. 28, *Whatever the position... poetry may be*: In the MS this paragraph is subtitled: *Accomplishment*.

p. 34, *Alchemist Theatre*: Published in Buenos Aires in a Spanish translation with the title *El teatro alquimico* in the magazine *Sur* (No. 6, September 1932). Jules Supervielle had asked Antonin Artaud for this text. (See Fragment XVII in the Appendix, which is interesting for more than one reason. In fact it explains why so many of Antonin Artaud's texts were written in letter form or were excerpts from letters.)

p. 38, *On the Balinese Theatre*: The first part of this text was published in the *Nouvelle Revue Française* (No. 217, October 1931) entitled: *The Balinese Theatre at the Colonial Exhibition*.

The second part is made up of notes taken from letters and various MSS. In particular the entire passage beginning: "This show is more than we can approach head on", down to "absolutely stylized", is taken from a letter to Jean Paulhan.

p. 38, *The first Balinese theatre... hallucination and terror*: The first paragraph in No. 217 of the *Nouvelle Revue Française* reads as follows:

The Balinese theatre show derived from dance, singing and mime – and a little from theatre such as we understand it in this country – using what are no doubt age-old methods of proven effectiveness, re-established theatre's original purpose, presenting it as all these elements fused and combined from a hallucinatory and fearful aspect.

p. 40, *one of the first plays of the Alfred Jarry Theatre*: The play alluded to is probably *The Secrets of Love* (1924) by Roger Vitrac (1899–1952).

p. 42, *This throbbing ensemble… artistic feelings*: A variant copy contains an additional paragraph:

My Dear Friend. I wanted to write to you direct, to share my enthusiasm with you and to show you that my article, perhaps not as good as this letter, was not prompted by fake enthusiasm.

p. 43, *Aside from this show's… absolutely stylized*: Variant MS:

I dwelt on the massive intellectual aspect of this show, which seems made to teach and surprise us by this revealing aspect of nature suddenly seeming to disperse in signs, to teach us the metaphysical identity of abstract and concrete and to teach it to us in lasting gestures.

p. 43, *All creativity stems… speech prior to words*: On a variant copy this paragraph is preceded by the following:

Balinese theatre fixes an idea of pure theatre in our minds in a masterly fashion.

p. 43, *This theatre does away… a double Spirit*: It seems the end of this paragraph and the two short following paragraphs were added by Antonin Artaud when correcting the proofs in 1937. Besides, one can compare the tone of the last three sentences with *The New Revelations of Being* written in 1937 before Antonin Artaud left for Ireland.

p. 43, *This theatre vibrates with instinctive things*: A variant copy contains an additional paragraph:

> Accumulated sensations of unbelievable wealth and abundance descend upon us so we no longer know what area of our sensibility or intellect to classify and put them in, but this spontaneous pleasure and sensation does not immediately take full effect. The Balinese theatre show uses a language of movement and signs whose aim seems to replace what generally belongs to words.

p. 43, *some of the mind's most secret perceptions*: Additional paragraph:

> Balinese theatre gives us an impression of pure theatre in the sense that it does away with the playwright, that behind the organizer of this wonderful collection of stage displays one does not feel the presence of a certain number of themes introduced by what in modern Western theatre generally corresponds to the author. Instead we feel this organizer, or if you like producer, his own author, his own creator, working with exclusively objective stage means.

p. 46, *divinely anachronistic… Other World in this way*: Additional paragraph:

> …divinely anachronistic and divinely unworldly. And I do not know what theatre today would dare to show the horrors of a soul [in its ascensions through the kingdoms and cycles of the highest moral chambers towards reconquering ultimate Nirvana.
>
> Yet this is certainly the subject of the Balinese theatre's last play, with the episodic battle between Fathers and Dragons shown by all kinds of symbolic representation, by the conventionalized costumes.
>
> The Balinese's theatrical sense reaches its climax in these battles just as these supposed dances turn into stupendous mime, metaphysics of mime play based, so it seems, on the subconscious's very shudders and trances].

p. 47, *Supporters of classifications... substantiated attraction*: There is another version of this paragraph, struck out by the author:

Balinese Theatre

Balinese theatre is a wonderful affront to our present-day Western theatre concepts. Supporters of archetypal classifications in matters of stage production can pretend to see in the Balinese theatre's magnificent artists some kind of sacred *dancers*, and that the aim of these dances and the religious, esoteric aspect of their origins removes them for ever from the norm of our profane life. The truth is that the Balinese theatre, contrasted with the pedestrian preoccupations without any implications, and the almost exclusively psychological object of our theatre, where besides, stage gesture is of little account and has no life of its own, any independent life belonging to it alone, the Balinese theatre offers us a certain concept of pure theatre through productions of the highest intellectual scope.

p. 49, *Oriental and Western Theatre*: Text mentioned by Antonin Artaud for the first time in a letter dated 29th December 1935 and in two letters dated 6th January 1936, all three addressed to Jean Paulhan.

p. 51, *Any true feeling... lose by it*: We have been unable to find the text from which Antonin Artaud took this quotation. In fact it does not exist in any published text prior to 1935 that is known to us. It may be a quote from a lecture such as that entitled *Art and Death*, given by Antonin Artaud at the Sorbonne on 22nd March 1928, the text of which was published in a booklet with a grey cover. Or a text such as *Point final* which was appended to *In the Dark* and printed at the author's expense by the Société Générale d'Imprimerie et d'Édition on 30th December 1927. Or even a text Antonin Artaud sent in for magazine publication before leaving for Mexico which remained unpublished, or else the magazine folded up – there are innumerable possible hypotheses.

p. 53, *No More Masterpieces*: Text referred to by Antonin Artaud in a letter dated 6th January 1936 to Jean Paulhan. We may venture to think it was written towards the end of 1933, since a certain number of ideas are developed in it which are to be found in a letter to Orane

Demazis dated 30th December 1933. See Fragments XXIII to XXVII in the Appendix, where the first rough drafts of these ideas are given.

p. 60, *Theatre and Cruelty*: Text referred to in a letter to Jean Paulhan dated 6th January 1936.

p. 63, *The Theatre of Cruelty*: Text which appeared in the *Nouvelle Revue Française* (No. 229, 1st October 1932). Fragment XXVIII in the Appendix may be compared with this article.

p. 63, *We cannot continue... reality and danger*: A variant copy contains a supplementary paragraph:

> We must restore the aspect of an engulfing focus to stage performance, to bring action, situations and imagery to that level of inexorable incandescence analogous to cruelty in the psychological field, at least once during every show.

p. 69, *In the Zohar, the story of the Rabbi Simeon*: The Zohar, the most important book of the cabbala, has traditionally been attributed to Rabbi Simeon ben Yohai (*fl.* second century AD).

p. 70, *The Actor... powers of persuasion*: See notes accompanying a draft letter to Gaston Gallimard dated 11th August 1932.

p. 70, *An adaptation... another play from that period*: Concerning this first show, see letters to André Gide dated 7th August, 20th August and 2nd September 1932 and letter to Jean Paulhan dated 7th September 1932.

p. 71, *One of Marquis de Sade's tales... the remainder*: The work in question is the *Château de Valmore*, an adaptation by Pierre Klossowski from *Eugénie de Franval*.

p. 71, *Büchner's Woyzeck*: The translation of *Woyzeck* Antonin Artaud wanted to stage was by Jeanne Bucher, Bernard Groethuysen and Jean Paulhan.

p. 71, *Elizabethan theatre works... character and plot*: On this subject, see letter to Jean Paulhan dated 23rd August 1932.

p. 72, *Letters on Cruelty*: The introduction to *Letters on Cruelty* and *Letters on Language* in *The Theatre and Its Double* is mentioned in two letters to Jean Paulhan dated 6th January 1936.

p. 72, *J.P.*: Addressed to Jean Paulhan. In the letters Jean Paulhan has kept, there are two dated 13th September 1932, but they are entirely different. It is very likely Antonin Artaud wrote a third that same day which he later recovered from Jean Paulhan to insert in *The Theatre and Its Double*. The second letter on cruelty is also taken from a letter to Jean Paulhan, dated 12th September 1932.

p. 74, *To Mr R. de R.*: Addressed to André Rolland de Renéville. The original of this letter must have been recovered by Antonin Artaud at the time, since this letter is not among those kept by the addressee.

p. 75, *To Mr B.C.*: Probably addressed to Benjamin Crémieux.

p. 78, *To J.P.*: This and the two following letters were addressed to Jean Paulhan.

p. 78, *Copeau's improvisations*: Jacques Copeau (1879–1949) was an influential theatre director and dramatist, who championed a more artistic, less commercial type of theatre, which encouraged, among other innovations, improvisation and naturalistic acting.

p. 88, *The Theatre of Cruelty*: The *Second Manifesto* of *The Theatre of Cruelty* was published by Éditions Denoël (Fontenay-aux-Roses, 1933). It is a sixteen-page booklet, with the title printed in large red capitals on a white cover. The booklet contains a yellow slip worded as follows:

The Theatre of Cruelty Company Limited

The *THEATRE OF CRUELTY* Company Limited is in the process of being formed. It will be legally formed as soon as an initial capital of *100,000* Francs has been subscribed. Persons henceforth wishing to become shareholders may send *M. BERNARD STEELE, Publisher, 19 Rue Amélie, Paris (7e)* as many multiples of 100 Francs as they wish to buy shares in the Company.

M. BERNARD STEELE will send them a receipt by whose terms he undertakes to deposit the sums received with the Directors of the company when the Company has been formed.

Once the Company has been formed, subscribers will be sent a copy of the Articles showing the number of shares to which their subscription entitles them.

A second white slip accompanied this first slip:

RECEIVED   from   M............................... the   sum
of................. Francs   to   purchase................. shares   at

One Hundred Francs each in the *THEATRE OF CRUELTY COMPANY LIMITED* (*Capital: 100,000 Francs*) to be formed as soon as the issue has been fully subscribed.

I hereby undertake to retain these sums in my possession until such time as the said Company has been formed. Once the Company has been formed, I will remit these sums to the Directors who will give me a receipt for same. A copy of the Articles will be sent to each shareholder upon completion. The Company will forthwith give notice as soon as the capital is paid up.

BERNARD STEELE, Publisher, 19 Rue Amélie, Paris (7e)

Financial Bases of
The Theatre of Cruelty

We wish to make it clear that the business side of this enterprise has been subject to the most careful consideration. In fact, any artistic undertaking, whatever interest it may offer in itself, is not viable unless one has studied the vital question of its material and financial organization, down to the last detail.

Also in order to offer the maximum security to future shareholders, we have decided to assume the working form of a limited company, the paid-up capital being set at 650,000 Francs. A short statement of the bases on which this Company is to be formed will be found in the General Prospectus.

In another connection, some details of what one has the right to expect from the company's operations are given below.

In view of the scale of the show and the size of the cast, we have allowed for production costs as well as the actor's salaries during an approximate three-month rehearsal period. Our estimates include payment for costumes, actors' salaries, hire or purchase of all stage props (depending on requirements), theatre rental, remuneration of the stage management, publicity, the cost of formation of the company itself, leaving a wide enough margin to allow for any unforeseen circumstances.

The initial outlay totals 650,000 Francs, which, besides representing the expenses calculated above, also represents the show's performance costs for a period of thirty days.

If one reckons on being only moderately successful with seating capacity *1,000* and say, *75%* houses, the capital tied up should be wholly refunded after fifty performances. Once this corner has been turned, the profits could easily reach *25,000* Francs a week.

In case this show should not be completely satisfactory from a financial point of view, receipts arising from an initial run of curiosity would enable a second show to be staged without any necessity to raise further capital.

However, there can be no fear of this, bearing in mind the incredible success obtained in *1931* by the Balinese theatre at the Colonial Exhibition. This show was launched *without the least publicity* and not only did it play to full houses for several months but the audiences received it warmly and people were regularly turned away, there being no seats.

Bernard Steele

Concerning the *Second Manifesto*, see Fragments XXIX and XXX in the Appendix; these may be considered as the first outlines of this text.

p. 96, *higher guna, the state of sattva*: In the Samkhya school of Indian philosophy, *sattva*, a state of creation, is one of the three *gunas*, or states.

p. 100, *The Marx Brothers*: A note published in the *Nouvelle Revue Française* (No. 220, 1st January 1932) in the cinema reviews entitled 'The Marx Brothers at the Panthéon Cinema' (but under a different title in the summary of contents: 'The Marx Brothers in *Monkey Business*').

p. 102, *Around a Mother*: A note published in the *Nouvelle Revue Française* (No. 262, 1st July 1935) entitled '*Around a Mother*, a Dramatic Act by Jean-Louis Barrault at l'Atelier Theatre'.

Jean-Louis Barrault adapted this dramatic act from William Faulkner's *As I Lay Dying*. The costumes and decor were by Labisse, the score by Tata Nacho. There were only four performances of this show at *L'Atelier*: 4th, 5th, 6th and 7th June 1935.

A text concerning this show written on the reverse side of one of the pages of the MS is reproduced in the Appendix (Fragment XXXI).

In the margin of one of the sheets of this MS, there is a first draft:

Direct appeal,
objective, encircled,
rhythm,
the horse,
death,
the river crossing,
the pubescent daughter,
a story narrated.

p. 103, *the sources of life*: Another copy contains an additional paragraph:

Who knows, not the gesture which connects with the mind, such as Jean-Louis Barrault makes use of with his powerful grass-roots sensibility, but the mind controlling that gesture, unleashing the life force? Even further, who knows that formless gesture resembling nothing else, which really ties and unties, where the likeness of the horse which takes shape is only a shadow at the boundary of a great cry.

It seems certain that this paragraph was cut from both the *Nouvelle Revue Française* and *The Theatre and Its Double* owing to a misunderstanding.

In fact, Antonin Artaud, writing to Jean Paulhan on 5th August 1935 about his proposed Mexican journey, added the following:

PS: What happened to the article on Barrault? The last sentence was cut! By far the finest!

Appendix

Documents Relating To
The Theatre and Its Double

(*Theatre and Culture*)

I – Words and the Period

Subterfuge for thought,
all our reality centred in them,
as to theatre, what a surfeit of improbabilities we battened on,
action,
verbal action,
the Word is the Word,
the Word shows the extent of our
Verbal incapability,
cut off from reality,
the sound of these words serving us deceptively.
Yet the value of imagery,
what we put into these words.

Enumerate them,
death,
fear,
action,
power,
dreams,
the limit of dreams,
   their appearance coinciding with our uneasiness shows their
importance,
   just how far they lead our thoughts
   to repudiate ourselves, to lie to ourselves, finding subterfuges for our
deficiency,
   touching nothing we could not arouse,

those words we use most often;

enumerate them and their flights,

yet, taken objectively, do they not assume especially substantial levitation.

The picture of false, temporary repose, its virtuality pleasing you,

is quickly transformed into perfect peace,

how does this rest originate?

* * *

II – *Preface*

What has our period come to,

Our period or us? We live under the sign of confusion.

The most important questions are raised,

vital problems;

alienation, collapse in values, everything makes us laugh,

no more love, no more suicide, yet love and suicide still go on,

more than one of us is gone but we remain,

this side of the departed, beyond ours (our lives),

we search for the sublime and our attitude is cowardly, we accuse the gods,

once more we are beginning to accuse the gods,

more than one man at a loss verges on the way, great words are uttered,

what is life worth; problems are restated,

our indifference in the face of our weakness or cowardice, we no longer suffer anything,

no more remorse,

even remorse is only a convention,

true we are no longer guilty, but it were better we were, for it would prove something exists, even the false ideas we indulge in and the ages reject, growing antiquated with time and entailing our guilt since we believe in them and they exist when we believe in them, but we have to believe in them to stay alive, since they represent life and we are beneath life.

Feeling all this, we think of theatre as a means of remaking life, whereas these means made people smile. This proves that those who are unaware of life may also be unaware of theatre, which catalyses confusion.

Life-manifestation: theatre-manifestation and cruelty-exactness, for it is intense, for life is present.

* * *

III

Chaos and Revolution.
Poet who will treat this order of events.
It is not his field.
But are there still fields, distinct from reality, which can be expanded on and organized?

That is the whole question!

* * *

IV

Theatre, knowledge of the body and *its* potential.
Not to get our breath back, but to *connect* breathing,
contraction and relaxation,
localized contraction,
focal expansion,
an identifying term.

* * *

V – Preface

The period in confusion,
a kind of dark ages like the Middle Ages, in events as much as in the mind.

Stupendous collapse in values: people no longer know what ideas to cling to, they feel ideas rot when exposed to the facts and man who does not conform to their ideas.

Beneath all this, poetry remains a diffuse idea of the sublime, only discernible under an overwhelming aspect. There is something sublime in certain natural catastrophes: earthquakes, volcanic eruptions, cracks in the seabed, excessive numbers of collisions, planes crashing in flames, railway disasters. There is something sublime and poetic in crime, in the nature of certain crimes whose motive is obscure, and there are many more besides.

It so happens we think there is a concept of poetry that must be dissociated and culled from written forms in poetry, in which a sick period in disarray wants to contain all poetry. I am exaggerating when I say it wants to, for it is really incapable of wanting anything. It is simply subject to a formal habit it is quite incapable of shaking off.

We associate this kind of diffuse poetry with natural, spontaneous energy, but not all natural energy is poetry. It certainly seems it must find its most complete, pure, clear and truly unrestricted expression in drama, and we are going to try and discover why.

I repeat the times are sick, having reached the point of madness where there is an overriding state of confusion before (either before or after) megalomania sets in.

This is not only because of a collapse in debased values, since values can no longer be corroborated by facts. Words have even lost any significance and we really ought to admit nothing has any meaning.

The mind searches vainly for forms, for a thought exalting it, and our age is searching for its own magic in the poetry I am referring to.

Without magic, neutralized life cannot exist, but even an age that has lost the significance of its words can still fear its terms, and the term magic is a part of that anachronistic heritage, although we no longer ascribe the same meaning to that term as in previous centuries.

To my mind, a magic state is whatever leads one to act, and we sometimes still use the term "magic" about an attractive gesture or cry, or a movement forms make in the air, a proof we attach virtues to it which go beyond its immediate, exact meaning – proof we have once again buried in our most intimate selves a diffuse sense of Magic whose charms only need to be aroused, afire with a burning, fleeting desire to awaken.

Nonetheless, this word seems to us to have lost its violence, its living, revealing virtues, and we still use it sometimes, but only poetically.

And we say "poetically" just as we would say "artistically", with that idea of useless charm, a pointless, ephemeral game everybody associates with the magical term "poetry".

Now we would like to restore poetry's dynamic, virulent meaning, its virtue as something magic. Then to conceive magic as releasing real energy, by using a kind of exact ritual. We would like to awaken those *manas*, that latent accumulation of powers concentrated at a given point. *Manas* mean lasting values, likened to the Latin word *manere*, which *permanent* comes from.

* * *

VI – Sacred Theatre*

At a time when everybody talks about culture without knowing exactly what it is, we ought to note the importance of theatre arts conceived as a means of organically supporting culture or renewing it.

There is the primal support of the body in theatre, distributing its breathing in such a way that we can geographically localize culture, creating a true organic hierarchy of understanding and feelings.

The family [...]

* * *

VII

There is an absurd division between theatre and life. We might say theatre began to deteriorate the day it began to command its own autonomy, to carve a kind of field out for itself apart from reality, a domain that betrays its unbearable artificiality. Yet theatre is reality's magic, an outlet for an overfull life that does not enter into routine existence, breaking the framework of visible, customary reality. It is the unseen transplanted right here, with all the abundance [...]

A game, if you like, but a superior game where a fragment of what is called living is involved. Ultimately, life itself is at stake.

(*Theatre and the Plague*)

VIII

Instead of bringing all your efforts to bear on an outward expression of scorn, an outward resonance of scorn ————

The crushing molecules cluster, uncluster, rush towards each other in blazing masses, in whirlwinds. Their inner gravitation becomes apparent, exhibits its crazy frame, discloses its multiple trajectories. All the hidden powers catch fire, are enumerated. The volatile mind animating them divides its [   ]* in the grip of the direst need.

* * *

IX

Gall bladder,

filled with a dense, gummy, solid liquid so sticky and adhesive the doctors who had opened up the body were forced to rip it out just as a dentist rips out a patient's tooth.

The stomach full of bloody irrigation, constellated by bloody sources spurting from many parts of the stomach lining.

The heart, arteries and veins were choked with abnormally dense, thick, sticky black blood.

But none of the organs were really affected, damaged, eaten away or attacked by the disease. None showed any real lesions and no part of the organic substance, the bodily matter itself was really eaten away, dissolved or dried up. Only the lungs were sometimes found to be gangrened, crumbling to dust, their matter appeared to be spoilt, blackened, to disintegrate, finally to rot, to become a mass of formless, gummy coal falling to pieces in strips and slabs.

But when the brain was affected in the same way, became gangrenous and rotten, it was solid, rocky, rather like coal crumbling to dust, or extremely finely powdered.

* * *

X

In 1894, Dr Yersin described the Plague bacillus:
Short bacillus with round ends.
Dye – aniline.

Symptoms: shivers, encephalitis,
dilated pupils, red eyes,
cracked, milk-white tongue.
Bubo, hard tumour, big as an egg,
tumour followed by carbuncle.
1. Red pustule covered with blisters,
the centre becomes gangrenous,
suppuration begins.
Pneumonic plague;
bloody spittle,
decomposition of the lymphatic glands, inflated in size and stuck to
one another,
congestive lesions of the viscera.

Momy, The Plague, Revue de Paris
15th February 1897

* * *

XI

If nations get the kind of government they deserve, periods also get the
kind of theatre they deserve, closely related to a certain kind of poetry
of events of a sudden, spontaneous nature, but including many things
and people. Epidemic diseases play a paramount role in these events,
and are essentially dramatic by definition because of all the powers,
events and emotions they violently put into play, without in fact using
them as absolutely as theatre or liquidating them as brutally as theatre
does its crimes, diseases and its potential, simulated scourges.

Now there is no finer example of an epidemic disease of a decimating
nature than the plague, a dramatic disease, a classic epidemic if there
ever was one.

Theatre and the Plague

If, as the saying goes, people get the kind of government they deserve, periods also get the kind of scourge they deserve and whoever wills it does not get the Plague!

* * *

XII

Theatre is not an art.

Art, in the dispassionate sense, in the sense of copying life, is a Western idea. It may well be a rule here on earth that the conditioning of matter ought to lie in this imitative inability, but no artistic production is of any value without the feeling of this inability, and the active, aggravated consciousness of what, just by being alive, has consequently been lost.

All mental activity is useless without constant reference to powers, without efforts which waste one away but exercise a critical faculty. True mental exercise sucks life as dry as a disease.

I see many (things) between life and the plague...

Art does not affect us. Art no longer affects anyone. If the body of society wants to deserve being healed this absence of any organic reaction can only be compensated for by its being organically affected.

Theatre must develop like the plague, that is organically and on as yet an undefined level.

1. From the point of view of physical and mental plague symptoms one might say theatre must reproduce them exactly, with a slight shift of emphasis.

2. From the point of view of healing the body of society, theatre must not be compared either with war or Revolution or any upheaval of that kind. We can get out of the way of Revolutions or wars through cowardice, compromise, concessions or other dodges, but we cannot avoid the plague, alone chosen by the mind.

3. Furthermore, from an epidemic point of view, the plague is the only disease exactly resembling art.

(Definition of the mentality of the disease: in the heart of poetry and theatre)

4. From a social point of view, one remarkable thing about the epidemic is that the disease passes from an individual to a social scale. Here the spectacle concerns everyone, strikes and violates everyone like theatre.

(*Production and Metaphysics*)

XIII

This fear which leaves us naked
something: what?
a theory of intonations,
spoken theatre,
psychological theatre.

What spoils Western theatre is its preoccupation with man compared with or(iental) theatre preoccupied with the Universe,
and because the latter remains steeped in the Universe,
its forms retain an echo of what motivates the Universe,
underlying these forms we sense the journey they have made to arrive at that point,
we feel they are near to breaking down and close to their origins.

Ideographic language is a reflection of the Universal. This is the secret of its magic action on us.

* * *

XIV

Theatre brings Marvel and Becoming, Becoming and Chaos together in a threatening manner.
To rediscover the religious origins of theatre is to initiate a kind of meditation on magnetism and on active, generating powers.
Yet meditating on Becoming is by that very fact meditating on *anxiety*.

And it is by no means axiomatic that the mental, organic arrangement by which everything in this world is channelled towards the senses *should be conclusive.*

A question mark is put after it, something is left open.

* * *

XV

1. 2 kinds of pantomime:
ideographic
where gestures are purely verbal equivalents.

2. We might say the mind, at the end of its tether, has decided in favour of the clarity of words.

But we must stop confusing the fate of theatre with the fate of literature.

3. Objections to words.

* * *

XVI

Their imaginary *Dragon.*
This dragon defines the disturbing life of inanimate objects by giving it form.

That world.
All poetry is metaphysical.
All metaphysics are anxiety and make use of fear.

Practise metaphysics.
Poetry of nature, of discharges.

Way of looking at the problem.
Stage language, when it exists and takes shape, is destructive, threatening and anarchic by nature; along with life, it evokes chaos, the

destruction of life, the abolition and sacrificing of those forms which herald all metamorphosis or change.

The usual definitions are discarded.

Chaos here.
Threats.
Balinese example may lack destructiveness, tempered with the crests of those forms about to flounder, forms spread out their veinous masses, ready to topple over.

Here also the temptation of space exhausting whatever presents itself.

Witchcraft profits from space, determination, *possibilities.*

To mistrust in their turn these excessive explanations, while trying to achieve the form of the poetry sought,
    if you called it destruction, you would in fact only grasp its bare bones, reducing ideas to one line, sucking them dry and finding them meagre;
    tell yourself firmly it is your own fault, instead of achieving a charged state, you miss poetry,
    while you could seek to dissociate ideas, you only end up *eliminating* them.

From language to reality.

The stage, the place where art comes closest to life.
Dreams of effective language.
The temptations to go from this imitation of life to life itself.

The finest art is one which brings us closest to chaos.

Idea of the uncertainty of our condition, of forms.

Poetry surpassing man considered as a provisional bearer of mind.

2 metaphysics:

indicates things used in an unusual, higher sense than their accustomed purpose without biasing their ultimate value,

pure, or universal metaphysics.

(Alchemist Theatre)

*XVII (To Jules Supervielle)**

Thursday, 17th March 1932

My Dear Friend,

Permit me to send you my article in the form of a letter. It is the only means I have of combating a completely paralysing feeling of pointlessness, and to complete what I have been thinking about for a month or more.

Alchemist Theatre

The difficult thing in European theatre's case is that if it made up its mind to be serious it would run up against tremendous scarcity of material from the start, and besides it was this very "scarcity of material" that led it to the point of inertia and exhaustion it has now reached. When we complain about the decline of theatre, first one wants to know who is complaining, second are there many of them, and third if [   ]* are capable of affecting the development of events, however little. If theatre lost all contact with reality long ago, we might congratulate ourselves on this secession.

* * *

The very name Theatrum Chemicum indicates that wonderful performances were attributed to distilled, convulsive material at the heart of the athanor, where each chemical element making up the composition of pure matter obeyed a visible rhythm in transforming itself, and evolved within a particular framework. It also indicates universal consciousness is artistic and contributes to giving us an infinitely freer, more tangible idea of art, a kind of untried idea, completely contradictory to our ordinary ideas of it. It substitutes an idea of organized, transcendental art for the passive idea of art according to which any concept is inert; which aims at making art simply a formal intent, fine attire intended to transform whatever it touches but is nothing itself. It calls the intellectual idea of a landscape "art", which might be *thought of* as being in a certain form while its total artistic aspect had been produced by one *single idea*!!!

In the same way as certain alchemical atoms in labour aim at becoming conscious of certain cosmic rhythms and that this active consciousness, not without some solemnity, restores the idea of a certain BASIC theatre, so alchemist theatre transferred to a human level can dissociate, isolate a certain number of essential operations whose special movement and curb conform completely with the genius of poetry.

If alchemic procedures are represented by a certain number of symbols that are always the same and whose effectiveness has really been tried and tested, symbols whose consequences are such that when they descend from a mental level and are expressed on a material level they allow us to *recreate* gold, we ask ourselves why we would not find poetic symbols on the illusory, imaginary level of theatre such as would lead to the effective apparition of spirits.

Otherwise what use are imagery and poetry?

For if the original idea of theatre is not to allow us to attempt psychological operations similar to those attempted by alchemy in the hollowed-out, empty excavation of the stage, that is, a small scale liberation of powers we forcibly constrict, it has no reason for being.

These powers must be intercepted in action, on an ebullient level, held, seething.

For example we can clearly see that a mind which dares to concentrate on one word, which in language [...]

* * *

Verbal language,
formation and the need for gesture,
what it represents.

* * *

There is no call for enthusiasm, lyricism, emotion or posturing,
   we need acuteness of mind, an accurate sense of moral values, we must search out the right tones and that search can be thrilling,
   actors and producers, in short all of us, must search for it together and keep telling ourselves that what is to be done pales beside what is not to be done,
   besides, the script is there and above all else it must be spoken,
   and I might even venture to say the script is so important that we ought to take no notice how the moves are carried out.

The author impresses through his power and acuteness of mind and we ought not to be beneath him in production; production disguised behind the play, almost mathematically; and contrary to the general notion it ought to give us the impression the author has accomplished his purpose.

And symbols,
attitude or poetic level.

(*On the Balinese Theatre*)

XVIII

Admire the sure, physical action of their show, admire a turning show which beguiles the audience's powers of sensibility.

Admire the show's indiscreet intrusion into the inmost areas of sensibility,
   the show acting not only as a mirror, but as a power,

Lastly admire that idea of spatial theatre, only truly theatre if it is spatial and displayed.

Bird flight, flexed,
rebounding from earth as if from a springboard,
it bends,
trembles in mid-flight.

The only nation in the world where a philosophic principle has found physical servers as well as a malleable, material existence.

XIX

[...] we can do without theatre,

where a theme's intellectual subdivisions are reduced to nothing and where *the intellectual space, the physical interplay normally existing between the parts of a written sentence are drawn on stage between the parts, areas and sight lines of a certain number of shouts, colours and moves.*

[Here the producer, working with all the means at his command, replaces the author in all the parts where in Western language we think we have to distinguish between a certain psychic content and its physical incarnation or, if so proposed, the production's conception.

But in the Balinese theatre's production the mind certainly gets the feeling that concepts clashed with gestures first, establishing themselves in the midst of wholesale ferment of sight and sound imagery, thought, as it were, in a pure state. To sum it up more distinctly, something like a musical condition must have existed for this production, where everything that is imagined by the mind is only an excuse, a virtuality whose Double produced this intense scenic poetry, this multicoloured, spatial language.]

Yet this concrete, physical theatre is tremendously, utterly intellectual.

This is the second thing to be noted about the extraordinarily rare quality of Balinese theatre productions.

The constantly mirrored interplay, passing from a colour to a gesture, or from cries to movements, endlessly leads us along rough, difficult paths for the mind, pitches us into that indescribably anxious state most suited to poetry.

This pure production theatre derives its own poetic reality, *based on fear*, from this clash of concrete elements, fully materialized feelings cut short in flight.

A kind of awful fixation emanates from this strange rippling of flying hands like insects in the green night, an inexhaustible rationalization, as if the mind were perpetually getting its bearings within the maze of its own subconscious.

Besides, the things this theatre makes tangible are much less emotional than intellectual, enclosing them with tangible, though almost constantly esoteric signs.

And we are led along intellectual paths towards reconquering the signs of existence.

From this point of view, the star dancer's gesture is highly significant, always touching that same spot on his head as he does, like a snake-charmer getting his breath, as if he wanted to mark the place and existence of some focal mind's eye.

[Even something which is a highly colourful allusion to physical impressions of nature recaptures them on a sensory level (as in the opening evocative dance) the sound itself being only a nostalgic image of something else, a religious state of mind where feelings are such, so malleable they are suitable for visitation by the Mind. Even the imitative harmonies, the sound of a rattlesnake for instance, or of insect shells splintering against one another evoke something like a clearing in a teeming landscape ready to hurl itself into chaos.] These performers dressed in dazzling costumes, whose bodies beneath them seem wrapped in swaddling clothes! There is something umbilical, larval in their movements. And at the same time we ought to note the hieroglyphic aspect of the costumes, the horizontal lines extending out beyond the body in all directions. They enter like giant insects covered with lines and segments made to unite them with the unknown, of which they appear as nothing more than the untangented geometry of natural perspectives.

These costumes which serve their abstract, sliding walk, the strange criss-crossing of their feet!

Every one of their moves draws a line in space, completes some unknown intellectual figure in the course of which some hand gesture concludes.

And the folds of those robes curving above their buttocks, holding them as if suspended in the air, as if pinned onto the backdrop, prolonging each of their leaps into flight.

And those death rattles, those howls, the rolling eyes, the unceasing abstraction, those sounds of branches, chopping and log-rolling, all this in a vast expanse of sound, flowing out from several outlets at once, all combine to give rise in our minds, to crystallize a new concept, if one might call it thus, a concrete idea of the abstract.

Balinese theatre reveals a kind of gestured metaphysics. It throws an uncommonly stunning light on the uselessness of language. And side by side with the mind, where everything rests on the equilibrium of reasoned things, it reveals another mentality.

Side by side with the mind where everything rests on a prolix display of the subjects of thought, it reveals another objective, physical mentality where thought is wedged between a slender, secret construction of gestures.

[*These metaphysicians of natural chaos dance, restoring every iota of sound, every fragmentary perception as if it were ready to return to its origins, able to wed movement and sound so perfectly it seems the dancers have hollow limbs to make the sounds of wood blocks, resounding drums, echoing instruments, to execute them with their hollow, woody limbs.*

I doubt whether there are many theatres in Paris today that would risk trying to interest their audiences in a soul's experience, in its journey through the highest realms of thought.

Here we are suddenly in the thick of a metaphysical struggle, and the rigid aspect of the body in a trance, tensed by the surging of the cosmic powers attacking it, is admirably expressed by that frenzied dance of angular stiffness where we suddenly feel the mind's headlong fall begins. They seem like physical waves dashing their crests into the deep and rushing from all points of the horizon to hurtle themselves into an infinitesimal portion of a shudder.]

For a long time now, modern Western theatre has given up scaring us with monsters, since we believe we would only burst out laughing at them. But we tremble when confronted with the monsters of the Balinese theatre.

This struggle is reconstructed by exclusively theatrical means.

B(alinese)* theatre has given us a magnificent demonstration of a certain non-verbal, completely extra-literary concept of theatre which frightens our Western minds.

This fantastically denuded, profuse gesticulation.

Purity derived from obscenity.

Ghosts that are engines, fantastic creations.

Our moral preoccupations are crude.

Our everyday psychology is crude.

Our theatre embracing and naming feelings is crude.

Here, this intellectual battle is reduced to objective, purely theatrical, purely stage elements.

A new sense of fear, positioning sound, knowledge of amplification.

Theatre of metaphysically intoxicated men, naked on a level with their intoxication.

The beauty of an interjection of rapture.

* * *

XX

Paris, 5th August 1931

M. Jean Paulhan,
Managing Editor of the NRF

My Dear Friend,

Aside from anything necessarily stilted, stiff or prearranged in any magazine article, even though written with all the required sincerity, I would like to try and convey a clear picture in as sympathetic a manner as possible, with a deep feeling of the intellectual comradeship, the strange mental, pre-eminently intellectual quality I felt at hearing and seeing this kind of simultaneous reactivation both of all our senses and mental faculties (so complete we end up finding ourselves unable to distinguish between them) that salutary, miraculous display by the Balinese theatre. To say that it gives our classic Western concepts of theatre a slap in the face is not saying much. It does more than present us with a surprising production, a surprising perfection of all the means employable in the restricted, limited stage space. Balinese theatre reveals the hidden existence of a kind of true stage language, so effective it even seems to do away with the mental processes that appear to have brought it into being, so that any attempt to express it in words is impossible and futile. It is a kind of concert of modulations and gestures, rather like the instrumental orchestra acting as its fabric or background. *There is a finality to these sorts of spiritual or spatial constructions, a kind of true physical absolute only orientals can show themselves capable of searching for. It is in the sublimity and wholehearted daring of their aims, even more than in the strange perfection of their productions that Balinese theatre differs from our European theatre concepts.*

Supporters of classifications and dividing into categories may pretend to see mere dancers in Balinese theatre's magnificent artists, *dancers entrusted with portraying some great myth whose very sublimity makes the general level of Western theatre so crude and childish, so unspeakably, disgustingly mean. The truth is that Balinese theatre offers and brings us already produced, pure dramatic subjects, on which the stage productions confer concentrated balance, a wholly substantialized attraction.* This impression is extraordinary. It is so strong that [...]

* * *

XXI

Pure Production Theatre,
mystic, religious idea,
these men reduced to a diagrammatic state,
their gestures fall so precisely; that woody drum music,
reminds us of those robots made of hollow wood.
Some speak of the excessive lavishness of oriental art,
but nothing could give a greater sense of being stripped
down, of purity, of essentiality...
Everything is ultimately, metaphysically needed, giving us the idea it
is rare and precious, profound stylization stemming from a profound
understanding of elements and requirements,
psychology is reduced to its ridges, its elbows, peaks, its need,
nothing gives us more idea of something pure, naked, detached,
they are steeped in deep intoxication restoring the very elements of rapture in them and in this rapture they rediscover the dry seething and mineral friction of plants, and secondly they restore them for us with the sound of plants, remains and ruined trees frontally illuminated.

All bestiality and animalism are brought down to that dry gesture, sounds striking the splitting earth, frozen trees, the lowing of animals,

their feet by that gesture of parting their robes, dissolve thoughts and feelings, returning them to a pure, objective state,

and always confronting the head, that cyclops eye, that inner mind's eye the hand seeks.

Miming, mental gestures, accenting, curtailing, settling, stopping, turning aside, subdividing feelings, soul states and points of metaphysics,

nothing could be more tremendously intellectual and exact than this gesticulation,

nothing more penetrating, shrewd or insinuating,

our psychological theatre seems crude, is ridiculed, ill used by *this quintessent theatre where everything returns to abstraction,*

their gestures fall so exactly on this woody, hollow drum rhythm, accenting it, grasping it in flight so surely it seems this music accents the sound of their hollow limbs,

the women's stratified, intellectual eyes, the dreamlike eyes seeming to see us and before which we see ourselves as ghosts,

the robe raised higher than the thigh gesture seeming to draw the body along, which continually takes flight,

the sliding feet which under the convulsive movements of the robes trace the body's intellectual abstract course,

utterly satisfying dance gestures, turning feet, mingling soul states, those tiny flying hands, the dry precise tapping.

This theatre makes our own, where feelings have to be specified, lived and played directly, appear so crude, where feelings are not outlines of feelings, the abstract features of ideas,

and where all feelings are brought to a state of consent, to a state of mind which registers and brings them to light,

where we watch mental alchemy creating a gesture out of a feeling or a state of mind, the dry, naked, linear gesture all our human reactions must have on an absolute level,

on the other hand, this theatre is a triumph of pure production

for to us, since it remains an inscrutable language, where only the essential in these gestures, intonations, cries, modulations and attitudes acts on us, we can be sure that what acts on us is not what is said but the way it is said, *and it happens that this way, this constant abstraction with its sliding alphabet, its shrieks of cracking stones, its sounds of branches, chopping and log-rolling fashioned in the air, both seen and heard in the vast perspectives of dispersed sound emitting from several sources, a kind of super-embellished language where visible signs are all that strike our minds.*

We can be sure that when, for example, Fear is acted out before us, modified, totally founded on gestures, postures and cries, the greatest dramatic authors can give up, having nothing more to say, since this is a matter of production and production is everything.

Who, after Arjuna's fearsome battle with the Dragon, dares say all theatre is not on stage, beyond words and situations?

Here, all dramatic and psychological situations have gone into the very miming of the fight, a function of the athletic, mystical acting of the bodies, the use, I might even say the undulatory *use (I will explain) of the stage, unfolding itself before us section by section.*

The warriors enter the mental forest slithering with fear. A great shudder, something like a prodigious magnetic vertigo overcomes them and we feel inhuman or mineral meteorites hurtling down on them.

The general trembling in their limbs and rolling eyes signify more than a physical storm or mental concussion. The sensory pulsating of their bristling heads is excruciating at times and that music behind them, sweeping and at the same time nourishing some abstract space or other, where a few actual stones finally roll.*

Behind the warrior beset by the fearful cosmic quaking, which may perhaps dissociate him, stands the Double giving himself airs, given up to the childishness of his schoolboy gibes who, also aroused by the repercussions of a fearful cosmic storm of whose rhythm he has understood nothing, moves unaware in the midst of the charms, the surging of a tremendous gale.

The compressed pain with which the Dragon confines himself to his corner of the stage, that distressing feeling of birth, a monster that will not come forth,

and when he does, the stage grows, amplified by all its turning movement.

The splendid humour, the delightful vulgarity with which the Double, who does not defend himself, does not reason, is unaware the soul is poised, thrusts the fleshly soul into the arms of his ecstatic master, then hides the whole of his face behind his hand so as not to see the physically necessary skylarking he does not doubt for a moment is taking place two steps away from him, and the humour of that fear with which his foot automatically strikes the ground with a repeated, accented loose beat.

The realistic side of the cries of fear suddenly introduced into this vast, certain, abstract melody.

And when the real, fearless warrior at last also goes into action, he advances on the Beast with a series of shudders, a rolling, waving flow, rushing in as if from all points of the intellectual compass, while a kind of sublimated courage closes its mental blinds on him, completes its gathering of cemented gestures, where only a quintessence of finally completed outline gestures remain, and dry crests of fear, bending over at times by leaps and bounds.

Here the genius of a kind of theatre that has gone into the body's physical trances is given free reign.

One really must feel the sublime airing of these gestures by which, in the midst of the paralysing ecstasy that will never leave him, the warrior wages a kind of war high on the summits of thought. The broad, intense waves, either of physical fear, now nothing more than the drawn-out shudder of an echo, or charming gestures suddenly learnt, unfurl and hurl themselves around the Beast, shuddering in its turn.

One must see the way the ecstatic warrior charms the Beast. He seems to say to it: but you must certainly know you won't get through.

Familiarity with sublime things led him to find the needed gesture without searching for it, and the fear he subdues is lessened.

These men are greybeards, why not Princes, intellectual rulers.

(Oriental and Western Theatre)

XXII

Because of the settled nature of the forms whose natural appearance does not unceasingly question appearances, because of language using gestures merely to make them say known things, using scenery as a framework and lighting to light the set; not using lighting like some subtle, revealing music, in a word a theatre which is not an act of witchcraft does not exist.

The theatre is ripe for crystallizing language, but this is not the theatre I sought *to evoke here.*

(No More Masterpieces)

XXIII

Useful theatre contrasted with theatre born under the sign of pleasure, relaxation and therefore ineffective,

theatre which does not limit reality to the concrete, to what is accessible,
with noble ideas of mankind, speech, the arts and poetry.
Such theatre presupposes a complete revision:

1. Of our ideas dealing with life, reality, metaphysics and universality,
2. Expression and its potential,
3. Active poetry, magic,
4. Human identity, mankind, morals, good, evil, sickness and healing,

a thorough study of the virtuality of art arises from this,
intimate and public poetry,
the meaning of occulting,
for what and for whom one hides,

the personal poet who wants poetry to serve him alone, and theatre as seen by that poet outside what he is in principle and in the accidental present.

* * *

XXIV

Art is not an imitation of life,
but life is an imitation of a transcendental principle with which art restores communication.

* * *

XXV

1. Richard II,*
our respect for masterpieces.
There are better things to do than to revive masterpieces.

For
2. Our ineffectual idea of art,
our literary, conformist idea.

3. Our contempt for theatre, a function of a conformist idea that the masses do not understand what is sublime.

The idea of what is sublime in life: death, dignity, heroism, honour, love, revolution, war and fear.
The masses understand the sublime or else they would not even be human, but we act as a screen between the sublime and all the masses, who are only conscious of masterpieces through our fossilized literary or artistic ideas.

Insert here analysis of the way we react to a singer, a painter to whom we attribute genius, an exhibition, minor shows and minor concerts,
without ever asking ourselves whether one of these artists or singers, once, even once, has ever been conscious of the basic ways of reaching

us, bringing us face to face with our most secret potential; first, our position in society, then in the world, finally in life.

* * *

XXVI

Plays written three hundred years ago expressing ideas, preoccupations, ways of feeling of men three hundred years ago in the language of three hundred years ago.

The problem is whether we are capable
1. Of recreating their equal,
2. Of forming an idea of theatre other than one involving worship of dead things and respect for written texts.

People pretended to despise theatre at a time when personal poetry was rife in a most disgusting manner.

We must understand that each period owes it to itself to express itself, and if it cannot achieve this, it must disappear.

There is no need to make long speeches to verify everything is falling apart and the time has come for all accounts to be finally settled on all levels.

I suggest something more, having become conscious of what theatre can do,
    surreptitious admiration for such and such an artist,
    distant admiration: (*word illegible*)
    Lotte Schöne,*
    once gone, there is nothing left.

It is time we became conscious of the convulsive nature of things termed artistic.

* * *

The main point: to see the relationships, learn the formulae, to find the right formula each and every moment,

To put useless, pointless gestures back in useful environment, relinking them with primal laws, making them conform with everything,

this minimum knowledge allows us to guide ourselves,

this model knowledge arising from imagery, linked with the energy inseparable from putting any formula into practice.

The imagery runs up against the obstacle, indicating it, and the obstacle, once uncovered, allows us to recognize ourselves in the interplay of events,

the experience of old age is nothing else.

To place vital energy at the disposal of imagery,

no more risky shows, impressions or risky admiration,

no more Surrealist or other empiricism.

This idea of vital energy placed at the disposal of vital imagery is valid for history to relate, for it must posit social and moral problems with a sense of the power and potential of which they are only symbols in reality.

* * *

XXVII

[...] the organism, and through the organism on the mind, using the same precision with which Chinese medicine came to know the sensitive points governing even the subtlest faculties over the whole extent of human anatomy.

In any case one fact is certain, theatre is the only place where the mind can be reached through the organs and for people as dull-witted as us, understanding can only be awakened through our senses.

Energy.

Psychoanalysis which [...]

the snake, the vibration,

either we will be able to bring all means of expression down to a kind of single, required focus, to the ideas underlying Aeschylus's theatre, etc...

(theatre a place of magic, the appeal of ideas and energy) magic idea of art,

no useless gestures,

or we will be able to stand a religious idea of theatre, that is to say without meditation or useless contemplation, to become conscious and also to be in possession of certain dominant ideas, certain notions governing everything and, since when notions are effective they generate their own energy, to rediscover this energy within us, creating order and raising the value of life,

preoccupations, ideas of things that count,

this habit, taking things at random, anything,

jumping at the first idea that comes along,

the first lucky scheme, the first amusing subject ingeniously treated, must end,

all these imitative methods, old tricks rehashed,

if certain fundamental notions, if some movement reactivating us right down to our roots does not go through us,

what are these basic notions,

if we think everything is subject to exchange rates,

that economic need controls everything,

that we are bellies first and foremost, which eat and demand food and that metaphysics like all precepts is in the belly, not taken as the sited, physical place of subtle preconceived ideas starting from there instead of starting in the brain, but as symbols of a purely material process, that the very idea of another kind of concept is just fanciful, baseless dreaming,

there are no grounds for going ahead and creating anything.

(The Theatre Of Cruelty)
(First Manifesto)

XXVIII

Word language belongs to literature, to which all theatre is subject.

A specific stage language must emerge. This language is contained within the limits of staging, giving the latter word an infinitely wider, more shaded meaning.

Enough to understand it as the language of everything on stage, that is to say not only decor, costumes and stage moves, not only lighting, inflection, psychological details of the characters, but everything stemming from a greater or lesser degree of outward splendour, aiming at effect and excitement, in order to penetrate the secret of expression in gestures and mime, inflection, stage moves and so on.

Inasmuch as all these elements act as imagery in their turn, making up a kind of expressive whole.

There are a certain number of topical words we cannot use now since their meaning has been so distorted. One of them is the word art. There is no worse, one might almost say more shameful job today than producing art.

The sentences I find in this way provide me with minor, borderline truths.

For this word now only serves to indicate whatever is bombastic and external in art, in a certain puffing-up after effects, after outward expression.

For we have grown used to making forms serve only to indicate themselves.

Not a matter of art's outward attitudes but its disgusting individuality.

Art is no longer opposed to language, inasmuch as it serves to indicate all means of expression extraneous to language, but…

The fact the ancient Romans used to be left seated all day on school benches,

Black benches, rough, unpolished wood facing the grey window.

To turn away from the everyday psychology of feelings (everyday feelings) to [...]

(The Theatre of Cruelty)
(Second Manifesto)

XXIX – Theatre

Unravel space in this theatre,

new idea of space increased by ripping it apart, unravelling it thread by thread, examining it down to the ligaments. Underlying it, extraordinary riches appear, pure Genetic ideas of the Cosmos in turmoil, linked and showing their filiation with the entire gamut of human feelings, belonging to a field called psychology,

a recital of these ideas characterized by their turmoil, their strength, must give rise to a powerfully lyrical, demonstrative passage, these ideas being recaptured alive in the torrid relationships between them and in whatever they disturb in fields that are not basic principles.

Staging

Fire, pain, groans become characters physically beset, the whorls of their robes expressing convulsion, exasperation and fire. These characters run following a rhythm and a speed expressing the inner swiftness of their pain and exasperation,

then, as these characters flee, as these inflamed men leap, inflammatory voices arise like cones of fire or geysers, echoing through several parts of the house on diverse inflections, and finally physical, accusing hands attack, mounted on the tips of battering rams activated by ropes or groups of men. These accusing hands and voices block the fleeing men's way in places, these mounted Rams attack the scattered bodies at length with as much noise as a pneumatic drill, the bellows in a forge or a smelter in a blast furnace, and succeed in pulverizing them.

* * *

XXX

We are all fed up with the kind of after-dinner theatre we see today, since it is nothing but an ineffectual game. We all feel the need for theatre which acts, gets to the heart of the matter. Without demanding documentary theatre, properly speaking, we feel the need for theatre which stops being a pointless art game unrelated to events, especially unrelated to what is deep and dramatic in our present-day preoccupations. We feel in a fair way to live events of the first importance not only on a national level, but on a European or world level, and even on a purely philosophical level there is something corrupt and unsure in all our relationships, and it seems theatre's role to reflect these disturbances and upheavals organically or spatially in vivid imagery. Besides, the discredit into which theatre has fallen today strikes at expression in general along with language, whether the language of the arts – music, dancing, painting – or that of speech, dialogue between lively men. In a word, we feel a violent physical need, like an organic nostalgia, for magic art and speech. Since theatre is the only art that can synthesize all expressive means and all languages, we expect theatre to restore the meaning of a new, vital magic reconciling us with it and perhaps even with life.

This is nothing less than a matter of reviving a religious concept of theatre, however down at heel the term may be, and to revive it not in the mind but in fact, to rivet the understanding and attention by objective means, by projection, by visual or sound explosions able to rivet sensibility in the proper sense of the word. Metaphysics, the mentality, the religious side of theatre, will follow.

Such a theatre's programme is double, as will be seen. We must:

1. On the one hand revive the mental impression of theatre, making it abandon its psychological lower depths, the sole source it has drawn on for one hundred years, to dig down into certain extensive sources, without which real magic, objective, effective poetry cannot exist.

2. Change the visual costume of theatre, its outward aspect, in short, its language. To revive the idea of spectacle and to renew it from both sides, that is to say, besides the magic, magnificent side of visual theatre, to broaden and protract the effectiveness of colour, movement, speech and sound to a culminating point, in other words everything which is expression and everything which is imagery, by making each

146

word and each expression and act a means of affecting, disturbing, dissociating sensitivity and particularly to isolate it from the mind and its normal diet,

and on the other hand, also to prolong and intellectually to extend the meaning of every spoken word and all imagery, by reconstituting and assembling them in the form of symbols and by attempting to rediscover the links between these symbols and a certain number of vital principles.

In this way the distracting side of theatre will disappear – that is, plays telling actual stories and narrating them as such – and the interjection of a certain number of forgotten elements ought to be a *sine qua non* condition of all expression and even of all imagery in every show.

(*Around a Mother*)

XXXI

Theatre may be a clash of gestures, words, movement and sound, but above all it is conflict, a call to opposing forces, shocks solved in time more than in space.

In Barrault's play there are spatial shocks but no temporal ones, so to speak.

Yet this is a religious show. It points to the reappearance of an ancient, religious mood in theatre, showing that *Around a Mother* has renewed its links with Tradition. But I repeat, if it is religious it is so by dint of applying itself, and because it renders a kind of higher dignity to human gestures, their most intense meaning. It demonstrates the beauty of nature's movements when we evoke them in an absolute light. But it does not depict the gestures of emotion. And what one calls soul does not enter into it. The symbolic vision in gestures applies above all to things in the soul, but the love emanating from this show can be traced to the body alone. Thus, to my way of thinking, if it is not total theatre, it is undeniably theatre since it recalls true theatre's ways and means, used with incredible success.

Certainly, when Barrault takes gestures or an acting area, he brings them to life, but gesture from the plastic aspect and space from a material aspect, and in so doing, he reaches the mind but never plunges into mystery and so we may say his show has neither the mystery nor the mind of theatre.

Barrault endlessly travels between mind and matter.

Notes on Theatre

XXXII

In other words; the liberation Frenchmen are concerned with will be more active because it comes from afar and will evidently be more unexpected.

* * *

XXXIII

And then is the important that important,
do I go to the theatre because I am bored?

* * *

XXXIV

Theatre is like psychic electrolysis in which the intellect must be steeped from time to time.

Notes to the Appendix

p. 121, *Sacred Theatre*: In a foreword to *Vie et mort de Satan le feu* (Éditions Arcanes, 1953) M. Serge Berna tells how in an attic which he was helping a friend of his to clear, he found some of Antonin Artaud's manuscripts. He chose some pieces among them eclectically and published them under the title of one of the fragments thus found. *Sacred Theatre* was one of the excerpts he chose.

p. 122, [   ]: A gap in the original manuscript.

p. 128, *XVII (To Jules Supervielle)*: This draft letter does not bear the name of the addressee, but it is likely it was meant for Jules Supervielle, who had asked him for an article for the magazine *Sur.* Moreover, about 20th March 1932, Antonin Artaud, writing to Jean Paulhan, added a postscript intended for Jules Supervielle. Finally, Mme Anie Faure sent us the following letter addressed by Jules Supervielle to Antonin Artaud:

> 47, Bd Lannes
> 18th May 1932
>
> *My Dear Friend,*
> *Paulhan likes your "Alchemist Theatre" so much he wants to publish it in the NRF at the same time as it appears in* Sur. *I certainly hope that the editors of that magazine, with whom I am in correspondence, will have no objection to this dual publication. As for me, I would be extremely happy at their publication. Enclosed is the typed text.*
>
> *I would very much like to see you again when you return.*
>
> *With kindest regards,*
> *Jules Supervielle*

A further fact confirms Jules Supervielle as the addressee of the letter. In fact, Mme Anie Faure provides draft letter to Marcel Dalio dated 29th June 1932. It was inside an envelope on which a note by Antonin Artaud seems to indicate it originally contained two letters: the letter to Marcel Dalio and that above marked:

Supervielle Letter, Alchemist Theatre

p. 128, [   ]: A blank in the original letter.

p. 133, *B(alinese)*: Only the initial letter was written down in the original manuscript.

p. 137, *The general trembling... finally roll*: Antonin Artaud noted the following in the margin beside this paragraph:

> Low metallic sound,
> low cymbals,
> re bou no te ou la la la la la
> oula
> oule
> re bou no tou ou lou
> oulou
> bounot oula
> bounot
> bounot.

p. 140, *Richard II*: Antonin Artaud read *Richard II* at Lise Deharme's on 6th January 1934.

p. 141, *Lotte Schöne*: Lotte Schöne (1891–1977) was one of the most famous opera singers of the twentieth century.

ALMA CLASSICS

ALMA CLASSICS aims to publish mainstream and lesser-known European classics in an innovative and striking way, while employing the highest editorial and production standards. By way of a unique approach the range offers much more, both visually and textually, than readers have come to expect from contemporary classics publishing.

~

1. James Hanley, *Boy*
2. D.H. Lawrence, *The First Women in Love*
3. Charlotte Brontë, *Jane Eyre*
4. Jane Austen, *Pride and Prejudice*
5. Emily Brontë, *Wuthering Heights*
6. Anton Chekhov, *Sakhalin Island*
7. Giuseppe Gioacchino Belli, *Sonnets*
8. Jack Kerouac, *Beat Generation*
9. Charles Dickens, *Great Expectations*
10. Jane Austen, *Emma*
11. Wilkie Collins, *The Moonstone*
12. D.H. Lawrence, *The Second Lady Chatterley's Lover*
13. Jonathan Swift, *The Benefit of Farting Explained*
14. Anonymous, *Dirty Limericks*
15. Henry Miller, *The World of Sex*
16. Jeremias Gotthelf, *The Black Spider*
17. Oscar Wilde, *The Picture Of Dorian Gray*
18. Erasmus, *Praise of Folly*
19. Henry Miller, *Quiet Days in Clichy*
20. Cecco Angiolieri, *Sonnets*
21. Fyodor Dostoevsky, *Humiliated and Insulted*
22. Jane Austen, *Sense and Sensibility*
23. Theodor Storm, *Immensee*
24. Ugo Foscolo, *Sepulchres*
25. Boileau, *Art of Poetry*
26. Georg Kaiser, *Plays Vol. 1*
27. Émile Zola, *Ladies' Delight*
28. D.H. Lawrence, *Selected Letters*
29. Alexander Pope, *The Art of Sinking in Poetry*
30. E.T.A. Hoffmann, *The King's Bride*
31. Ann Radcliffe, *The Italian*
32. Prosper Mérimée, *A Slight Misunderstanding*
33. Giacomo Leopardi, *Canti*
34. Giovanni Boccaccio, *Decameron*
35. Annette von Droste-Hülshoff, *The Jew's Beech*
36. Stendhal, *Life of Rossini*
37. Eduard Mörike, *Mozart's Journey to Prague*
38. Jane Austen, *Love and Friendship*
39. Leo Tolstoy, *Anna Karenina*
40. Ivan Bunin, *Dark Avenues*
41. Nathaniel Hawthorne, *The Scarlet Letter*

42. Sadeq Hedayat, *Three Drops of Blood*
43. Alexander Trocchi, *Young Adam*
44. Oscar Wilde, *The Decay of Lying*
45. Mikhail Bulgakov, *The Master and Margarita*
46. Sadeq Hedayat, *The Blind Owl*
47. Alain Robbe-Grillet, *Jealousy*
48. Marguerite Duras, *Moderato Cantabile*
49. Raymond Roussel, *Locus Solus*
50. Alain Robbe-Grillet, *In the Labyrinth*
51. Daniel Defoe, *Robinson Crusoe*
52. Robert Louis Stevenson, *Treasure Island*
53. Ivan Bunin, *The Village*
54. Alain Robbe-Grillet, *The Voyeur*
55. Franz Kafka, *Dearest Father*
56. Geoffrey Chaucer, *Canterbury Tales*
57. Ambrose Bierce, *The Monk and the Hangman's Daughter*
58. Fyodor Dostoevsky, *Winter Notes on Summer Impressions*
59. Bram Stoker, *Dracula*
60. Mary Shelley, *Frankenstein*
61. Johann Wolfgang von Goethe, *Elective Affinities*
62. Marguerite Duras, *The Sailor from Gibraltar*
63. Robert Graves, *Lars Porsena*
64. Napoleon Bonaparte, *Aphorisms and Thoughts*
65. Joseph von Eichendorff, *Memoirs of a Good-for-Nothing*
66. Adelbert von Chamisso, *Peter Schlemihl*
67. Pedro Antonio de Alarcón, *The Three-Cornered Hat*
68. Jane Austen, *Persuasion*
69. Dante Alighieri, *Rime*
70. Anton Chekhov, *The Woman in the Case and Other Stories*
71. Mark Twain, *The Diaries of Adam and Eve*
72. Jonathan Swift, *Gulliver's Travels*
73. Joseph Conrad, *Heart of Darkness*
74. Gottfried Keller, *A Village Romeo and Juliet*
75. Raymond Queneau, *Exercises in Style*
76. Georg Büchner, *Lenz*
77. Giovanni Boccaccio, *Life of Dante*
78. Jane Austen, *Mansfield Park*
79. E.T.A. Hoffmann, *The Devil's Elixirs*
80. Claude Simon, *The Flanders Road*
81. Raymond Queneau, *The Flight of Icarus*
82. Niccolò Machiavelli, *The Prince*
83. Mikhail Lermontov, *A Hero of our Time*
84. Henry Miller, *Black Spring*
85. Victor Hugo, *The Last Day of a Condemned Man*
86. D.H. Lawrence, *Paul Morel*
87. Mikhail Bulgakov, *The Life of Monsieur de Molière*
88. Leo Tolstoy, *Three Novellas*
89. Stendhal, *Travels in the South of France*
90. Wilkie Collins, *The Woman in White*
91. Alain Robbe-Grillet, *Erasers*
92. Iginio Ugo Tarchetti, *Fosca*
93. D.H. Lawrence, *The Fox*
94. Borys Conrad, *My Father Joseph Conrad*
95. James De Mille, *A Strange Manuscript Found in a Copper Cylinder*
96. Émile Zola, *Dead Men Tell No Tales*

97. Alexander Pushkin, *Ruslan and Lyudmila*
98. Lewis Carroll, *Alice's Adventures Under Ground*
99. James Hanley, *The Closed Harbour*
100. Thomas De Quincey, *On Murder Considered as One of the Fine Arts*
101. Jonathan Swift, *The Wonderful Wonder of Wonders*
102. Petronius, *Satyricon*
103. Louis-Ferdinand Céline, *Death on Credit*
104. Jane Austen, *Northanger Abbey*
105. W.B. Yeats, *Selected Poems*
106. Antonin Artaud, *The Theatre and Its Double*
107. Louis-Ferdinand Céline, *Journey to the End of the Night*
108. Ford Madox Ford, *The Good Soldier*
109. Leo Tolstoy, *Childhood, Boyhood, Youth*
110. Guido Cavalcanti, *Complete Poems*
111. Charles Dickens, *Hard Times*
112. Charles Baudelaire and Théophile Gautier, *Hashish, Wine, Opium*
113. Charles Dickens, *Haunted House*
114. Ivan Turgenev, *Fathers and Children*
115. Dante Alighieri, *Inferno*
116. Gustave Flaubert, *Madame Bovary*
117. Alexander Trocchi, *Man at Leisure*
118. Alexander Pushkin, *Boris Godunov and Little Tragedies*
119. Miguel de Cervantes, *Don Quixote*
120. Mark Twain, *Huckleberry Finn*
121. Charles Baudelaire, *Paris Spleen*
122. Fyodor Dostoevsky, *The Idiot*
123. René de Chateaubriand, *Atala and René*
124. Mikhail Bulgakov, *Diaboliad*
125. Goerge Eliot, *Middlemarch*
126. Edmondo De Amicis, *Constantinople*
127. Petrarch, *Secretum*
128. Johann Wolfgang von Goethe, *The Sorrows of Young Werther*
129. Alexander Pushkin, *Eugene Onegin*
130. Fyodor Dostoevsky, *Notes from Underground*
131. Luigi Pirandello, *Plays Vol. 1*
132. Jules Renard, *Histoires Naturelles*
133. Gustave Flaubert, *The Dictionary of Received Ideas*
134. Charles Dickens, *The Life of Our Lord*
135. D.H. Lawrence, *The Lost Girl*
136. Benjamin Constant, *The Red Notebook*
137. Raymond Queneau, *We Always Treat Women too Well*
138. Alexander Trocchi, *Cain's Book*
139. Raymond Roussel, *Impressions of Africa*
140. Llewelyn Powys, *A Struggle for Life*
141. Nikolai Gogol, *How the Two Ivans Quarrelled*
142. F. Scott Fitzgerald, *The Great Gatsby*
143. Jonathan Swift, *Directions to Servants*
144. Dante Alighieri, *Purgatory*
145. Mikhail Bulgakov, *A Young Doctor's Notebook*
146. Sergei Dovlatov, *The Suitcase*
147. Leo Tolstoy, *Hadji Murat*
148. Jonathan Swift, *The Battle of the Books*
149. F. Scott Fitzgerald, *Tender Is the Night*
150. Alexander Pushkin, *The Queen of Spades and Other Short Fiction*
151. Raymond Queneau, *The Sunday of Life*

152. Herman Melville, *Moby Dick*
153. Mikhail Bulgakov, *The Fatal Eggs*
154. Antonia Pozzi, *Poems*
155. Johann Wolfgang von Goethe, *Wilhelm Meister*
156. Anton Chekhov, *The Story of a Nobody*
157. Fyodor Dostoevsky, *Poor People*
158. Leo Tolstoy, *The Death of Ivan Ilyich*
159. Dante Alighieri, *Vita nuova*
160. Arthur Conan Doyle, *The Tragedy of Korosko*
161. Franz Kafka, *Letters to Friends, Family and Editors*
162. Mark Twain, *The Adventures of Tom Sawyer*
163. Erich Fried, *Love Poems*
164. Antonin Artaud, *Selected Works*
165. Charles Dickens, *Oliver Twist*
166. Sergei Dovlatov, *The Zone*
167. Louis-Ferdinand Céline, *Guignol's Band*
168. Mikhail Bulgakov, *A Dog's Heart*
169. Rayner Heppenstall, *The Blaze of Noon*
170. Fyodor Dostoevsky, *The Crocodile*
171. Anton Chekhov, *The Death of a Civil Servant*
172. Georg Kaiser, *Plays Vol. 2*
173. Tristan Tzara, *Seven Dada Manifestos* and *Lampisteries*
174. Frank Wedekind, *The Lulu Plays and Other Sex Tragedies*
175. Frank Wedekind, *Spring Awakening*
176. Fyodor Dostoevsky, *The Gambler*
177. Prosper Mérimée, *The Etruscan Vase and Other Stories*
178. Edgar Allan Poe, *Tales of the Supernatural*
179. Virginia Woolf, *To the Lighthouse*
180. F. Scott Fitzgerald, *The Beautiful and Damned*
181. James Joyce, *Dubliners*
182. Alexander Pushkin, *The Captain's Daughter*
183. Sherwood Anderson, *Winesburg Ohio*
184. James Joyce, *Ulysses*
185. Ivan Turgenev, *Faust*
186. Virginia Woolf, *Mrs Dalloway*
187. Paul Scarron, *The Comical Romance*
188. Sergei Dovlatov, *Pushkin Hills*
189. F. Scott Fitzgerald, *This Side of Paradise*
190. Alexander Pushkin, *Complete Lyrical Poems*
191. Luigi Pirandello, *Plays Vol. 2*
192. Ivan Turgenev, *Rudin*
193. Raymond Radiguet, *Cheeks on Fire*
194. Vladimir Odoevsky, *Two Days in the Life of the Terrestrial Globe*
195. Copi, *Four Plays*
196. Iginio Ugo Tarchetti, *Fantastic Tales*
197. Louis-Ferdinand Céline, *London Bridge*
198. Mikhail Bulgakov, *The White Guard*
199. George Bernard Shaw, *The Intelligent Woman's Guide*
200. Charles Dickens, *Supernatural Short Stories*
201. Dante Alighieri, *The Divine Comedy*

To order any of our titles and for up-to-date information about our current and forthcoming publications, please visit our website at:

www.almaclassics.com